AF473984

A Book of Birds

by Humphrey Ocean

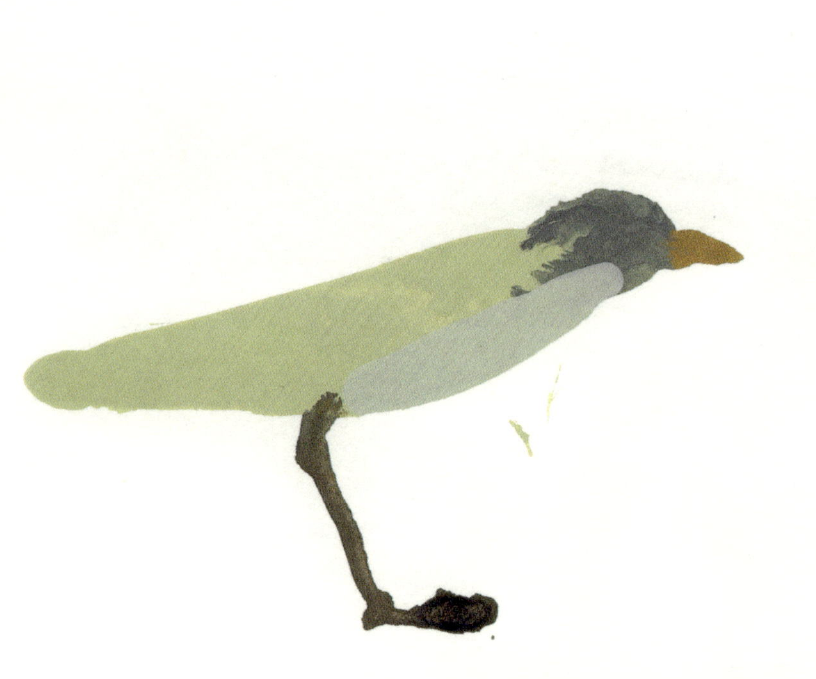

A Book of Birds

by Humphrey Ocean

Royal Academy of Arts

In 1993 I saw a puffin and that was it. Before that my life had been silent spring, so to speak. I am not a very good identifier (the bird has to come and peck open my guidebook and lie in profile next to its image) but the dusky, feathery, often earthy, sometimes startlingly colourful, sometimes muddily drab, nearly always quick quality of these creatures improves things for me. Just sitting still will do it, sometimes with reeds or moss or the flatness of water, waiting for a snipe or once every three years a rail. So far no bittern but you never know. A coot and the unsung mallard are their equal. As for song, very little beats a blackbird. These are a few of the birds I have seen, here in England and some in African hedgerows when I go and see my sister Rachel who, on the quiet, has loved birds all her life. This is not a guide, it is the imprint the bird makes on me before it's off.

I dedicate this book to Jennifer and Clive Davies who took me to Bempton Cliffs the day I first saw that puffin.

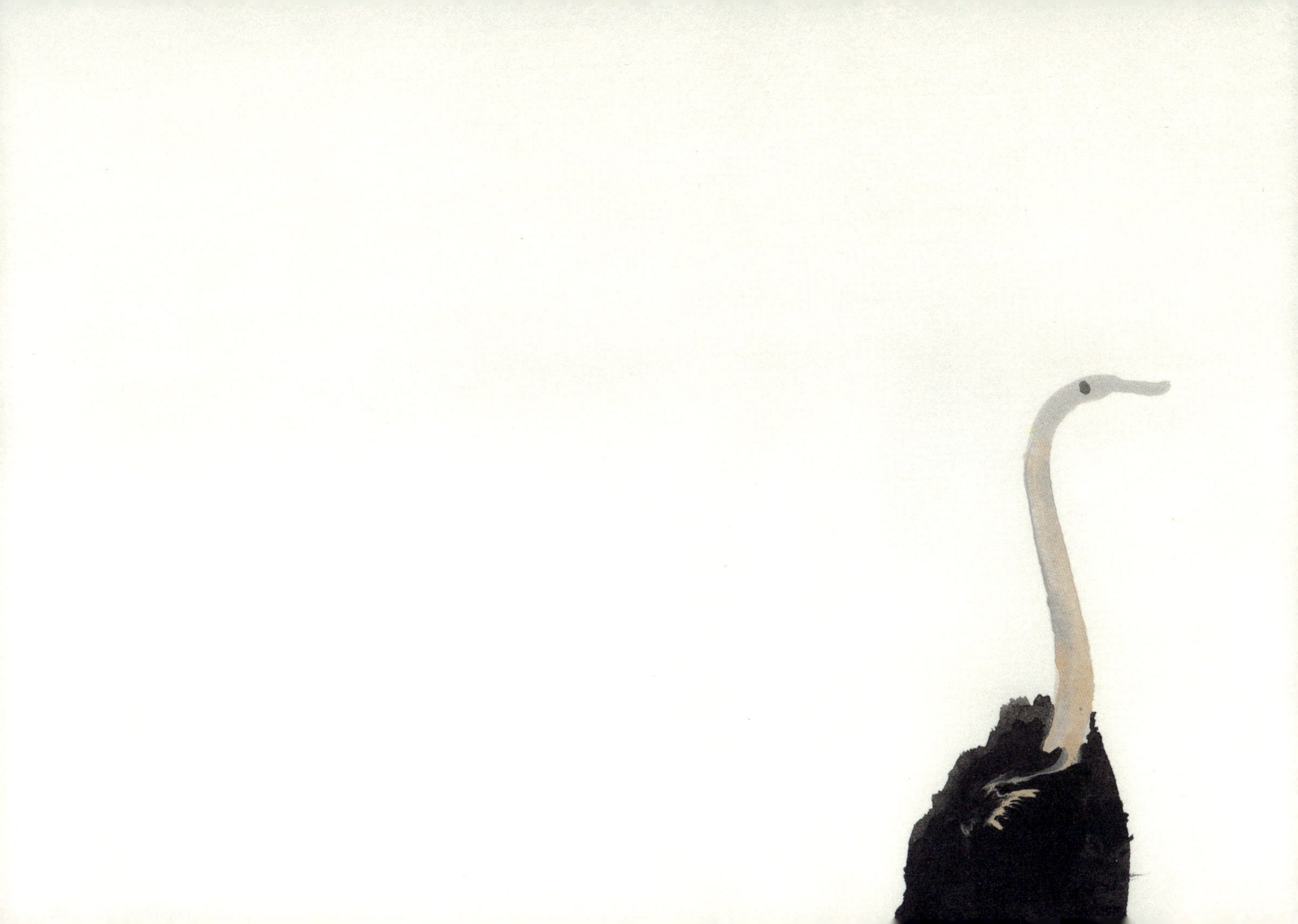

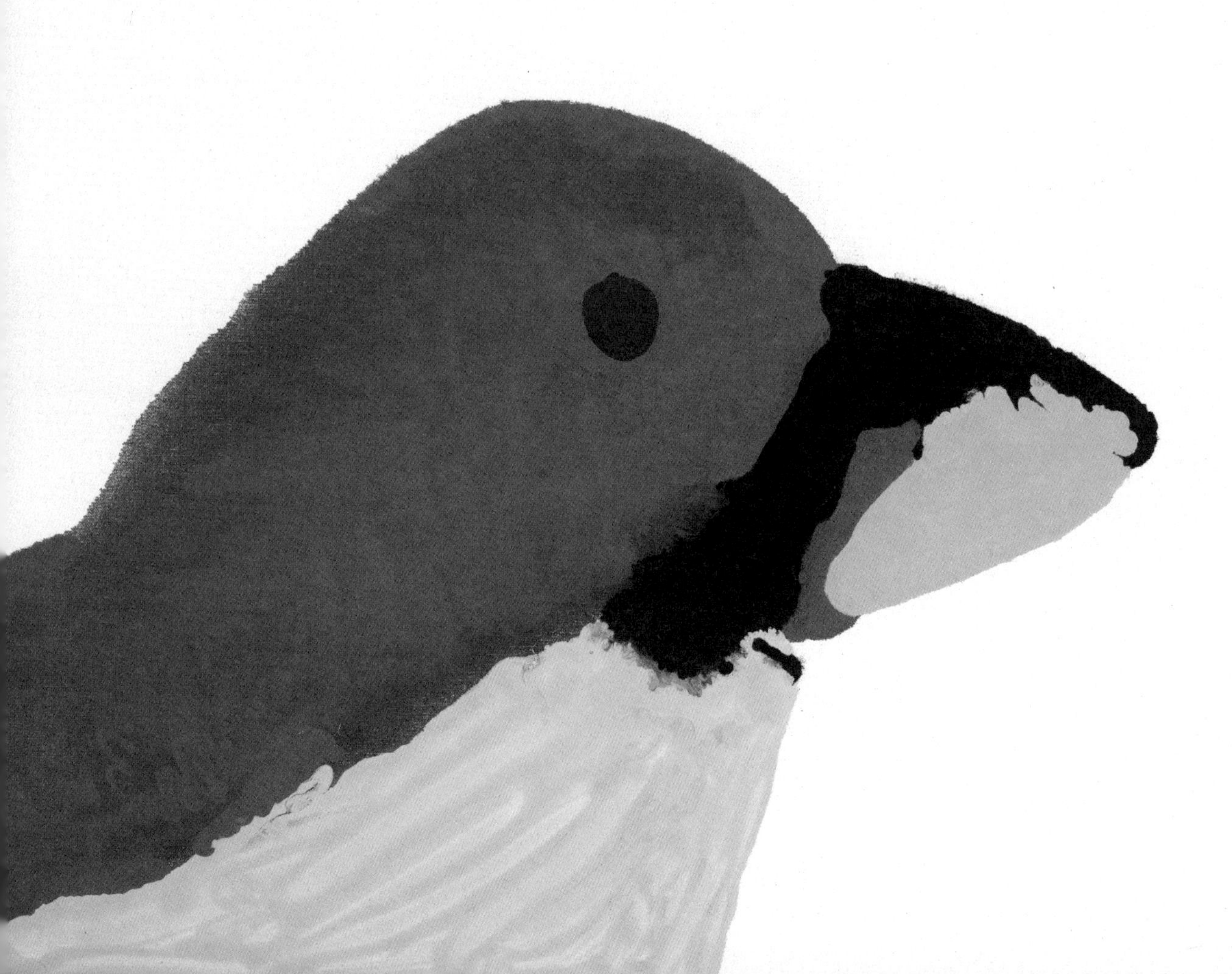

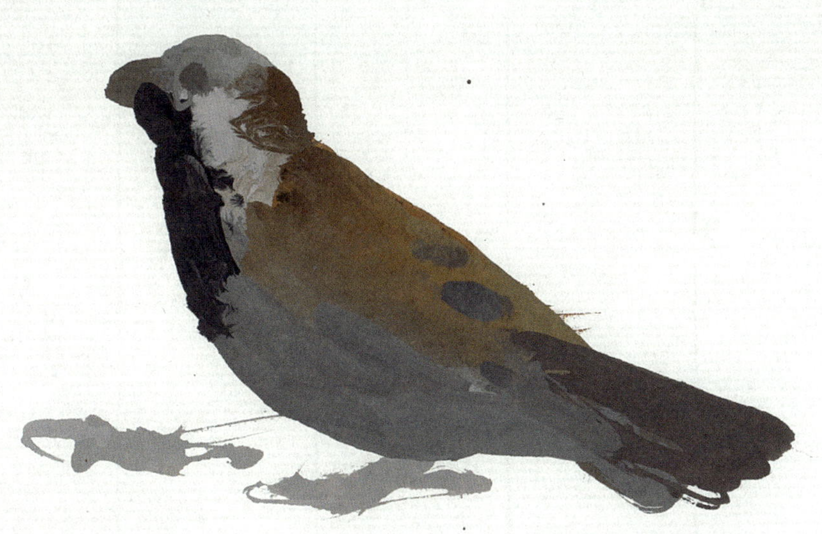

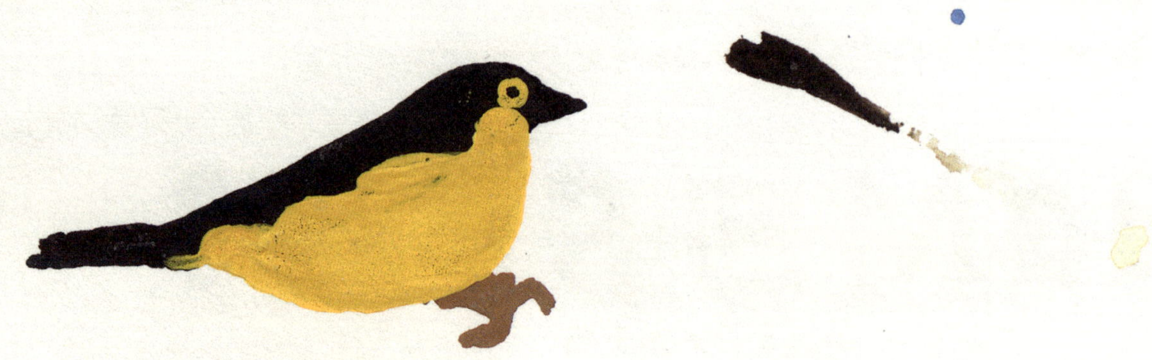

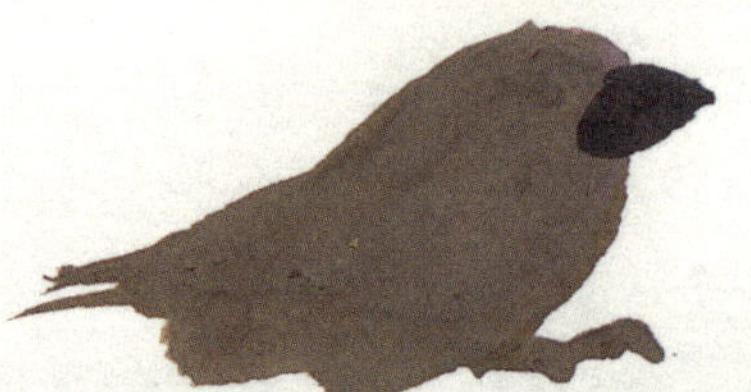

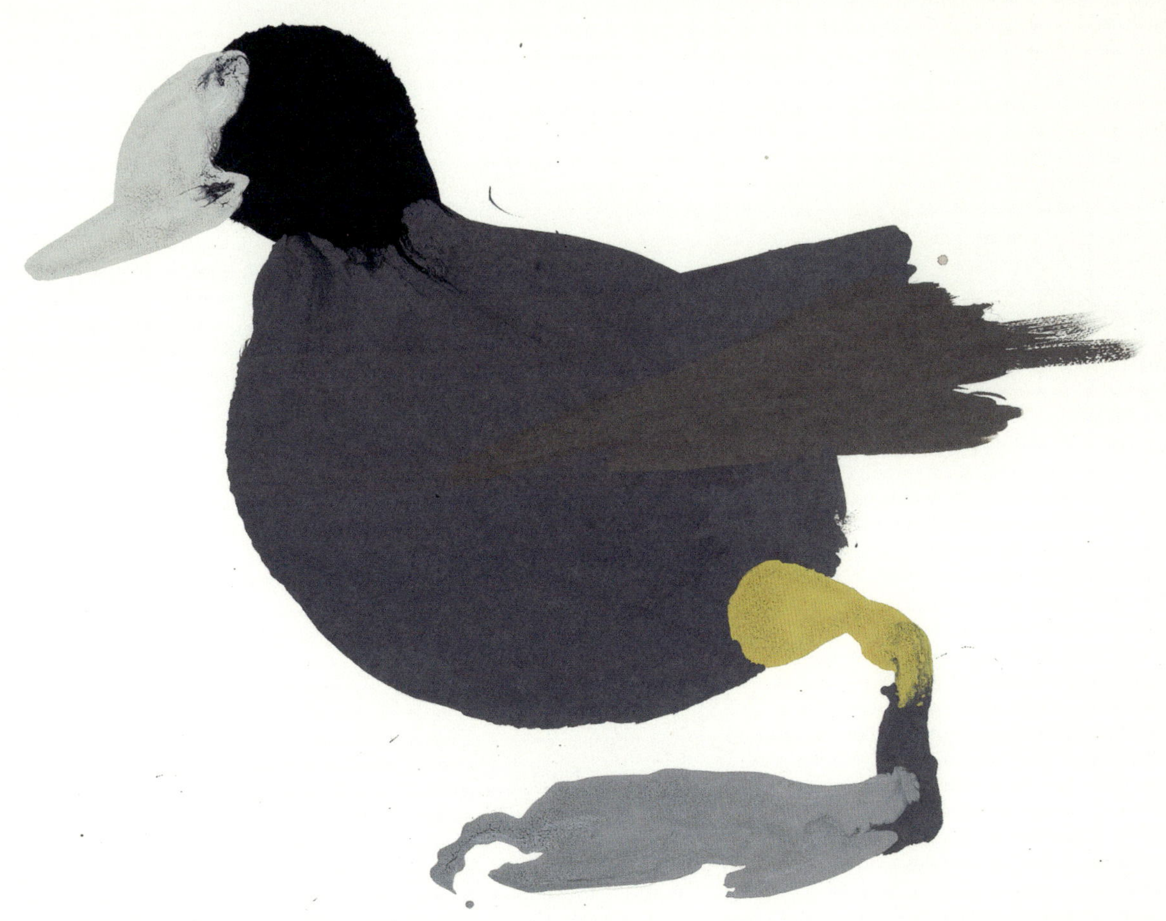

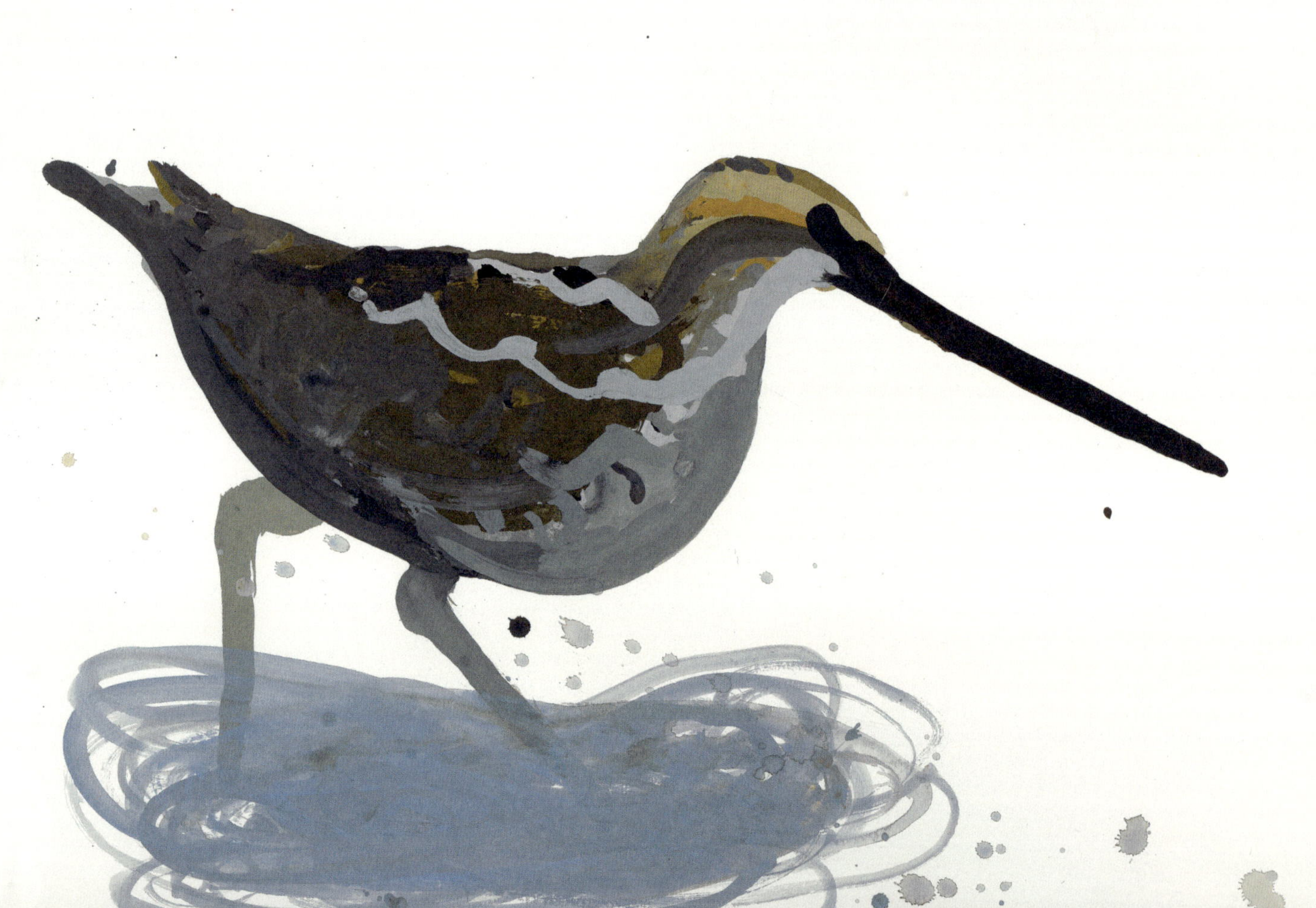

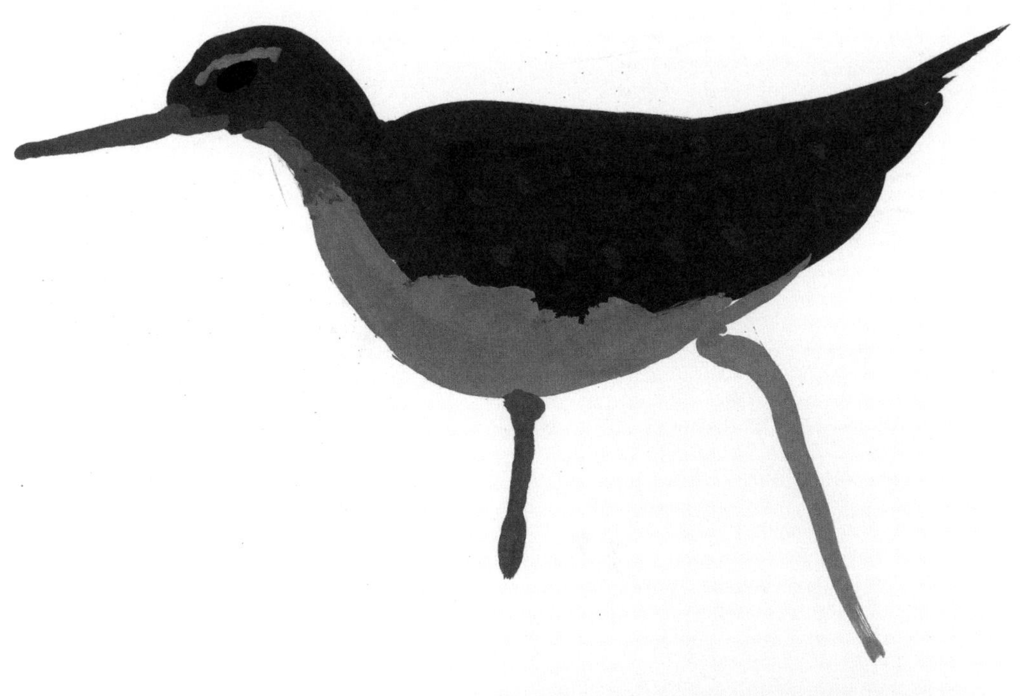

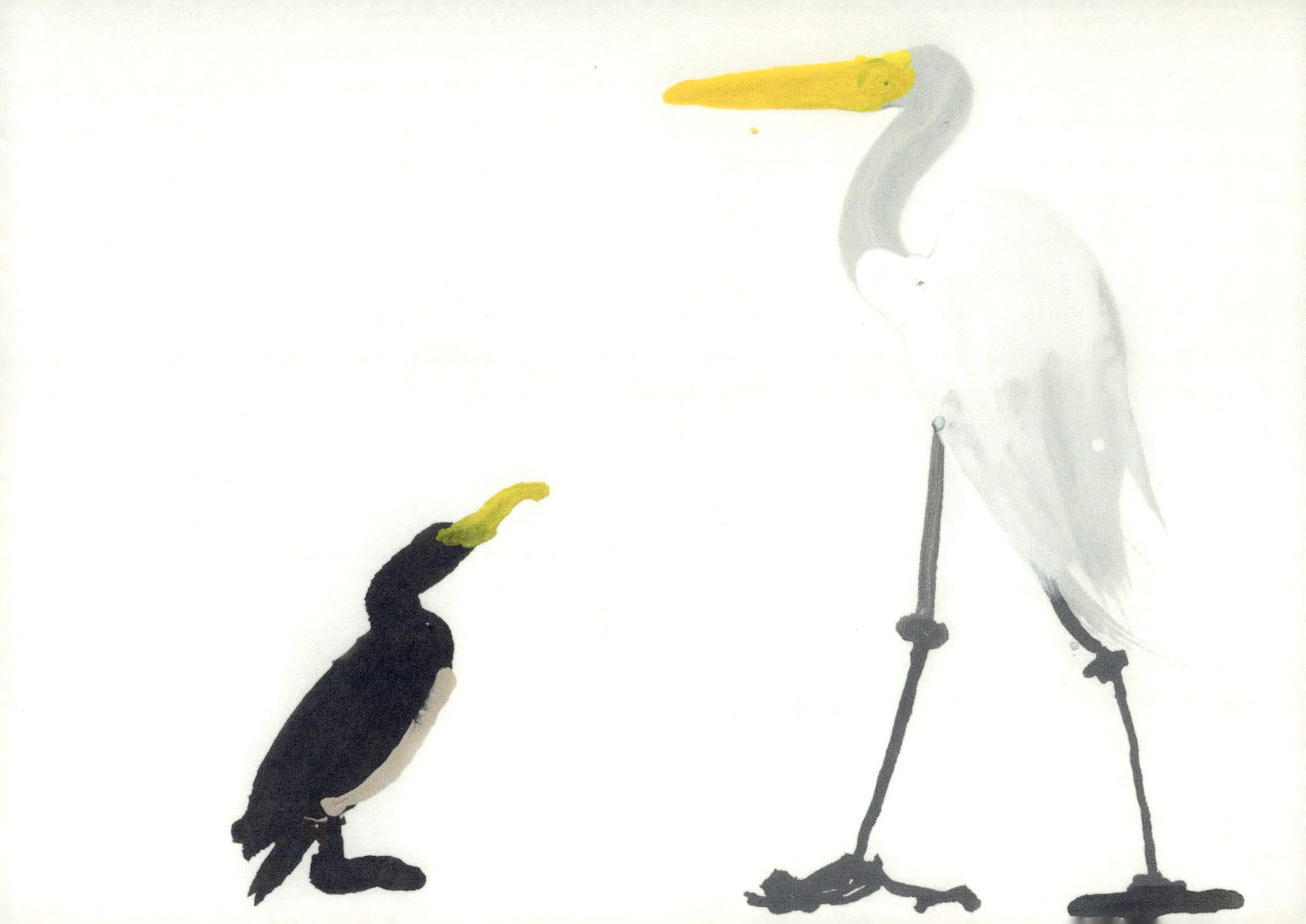

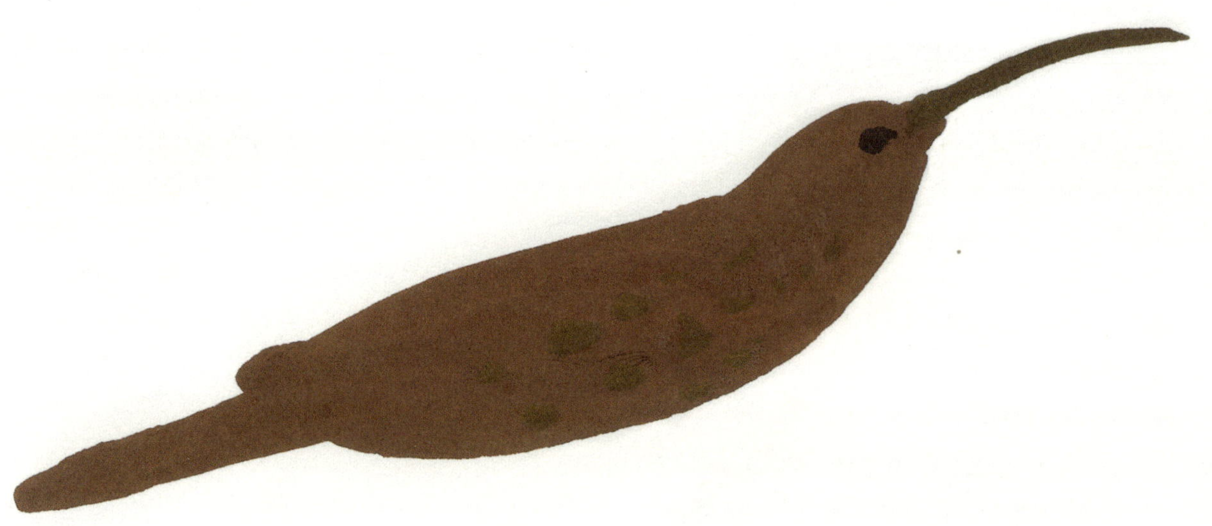

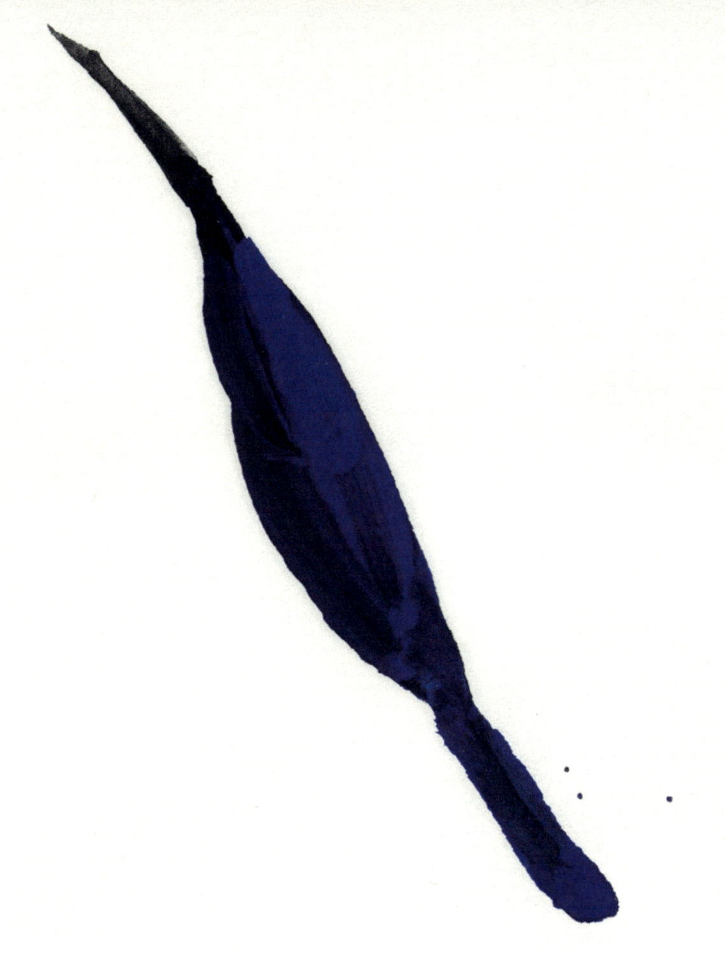

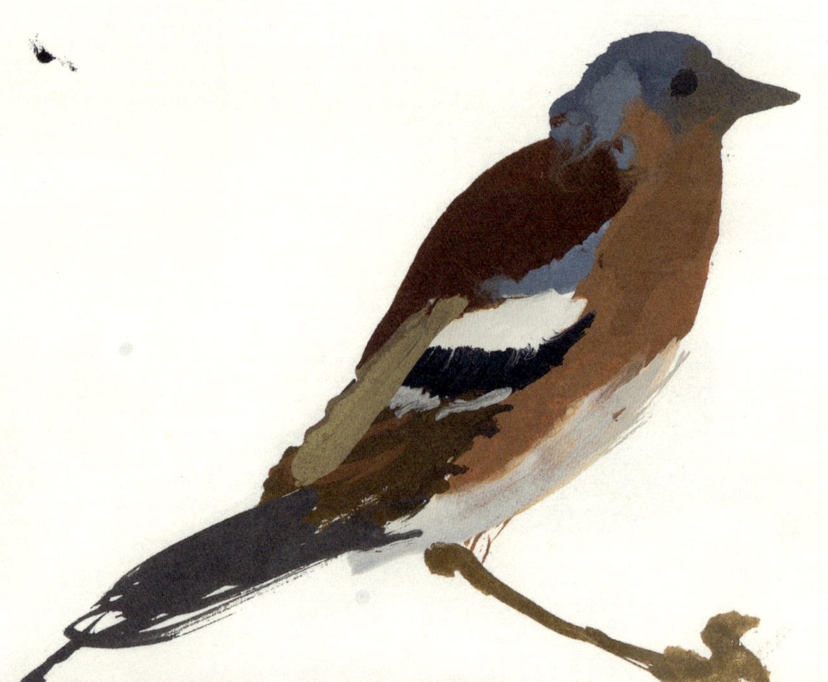

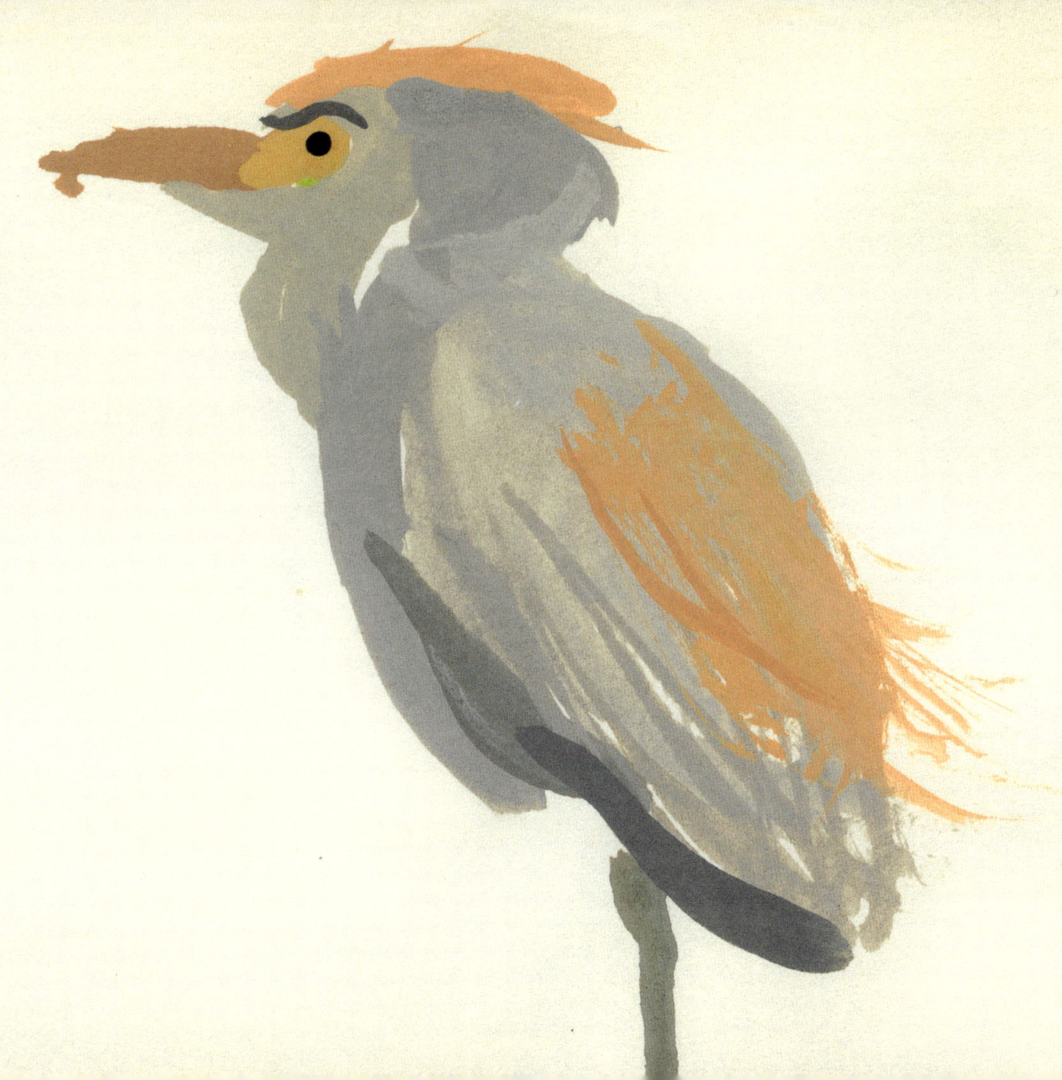

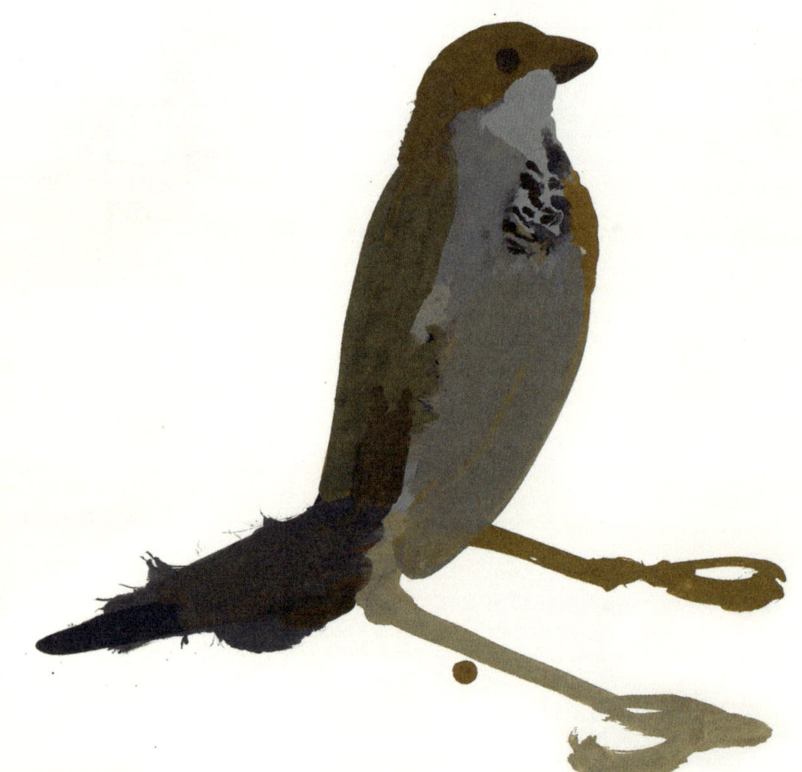

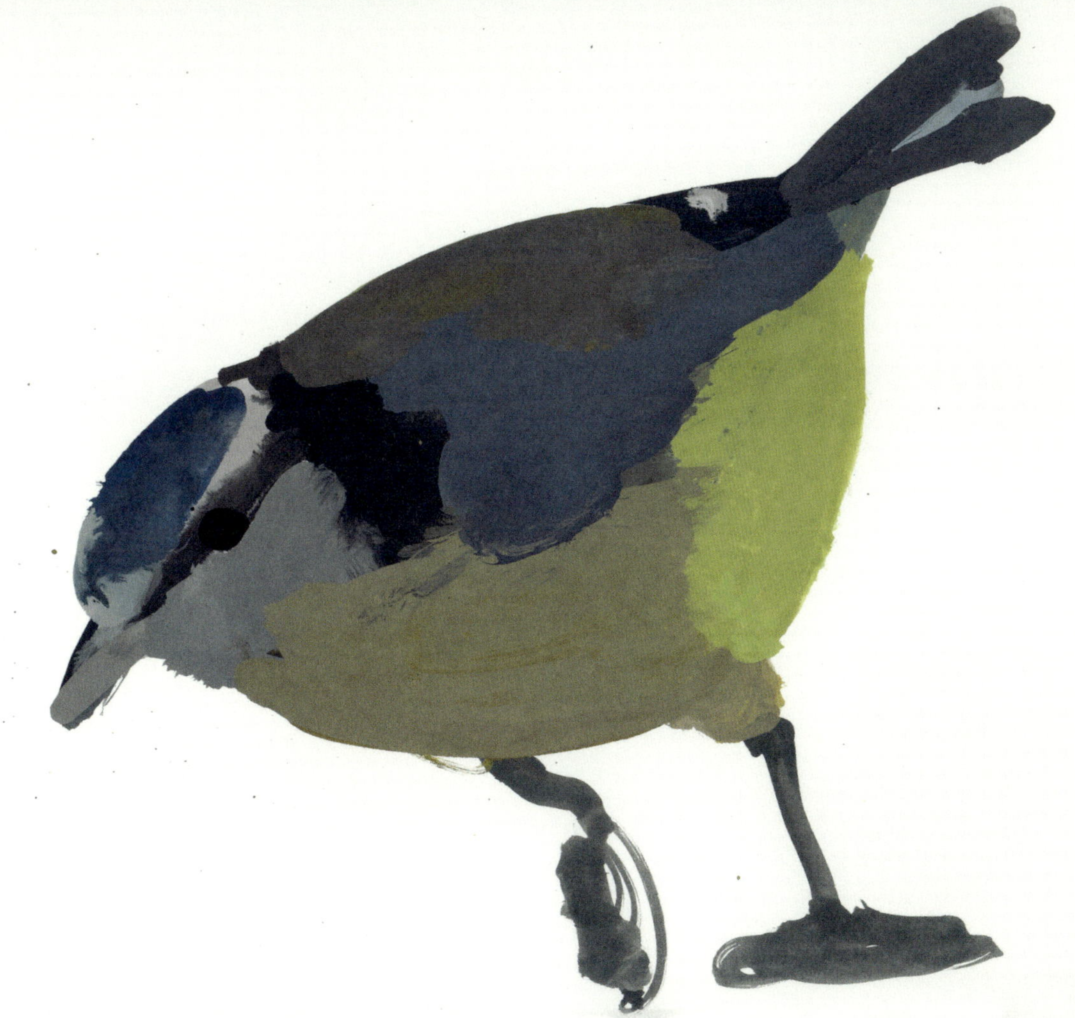

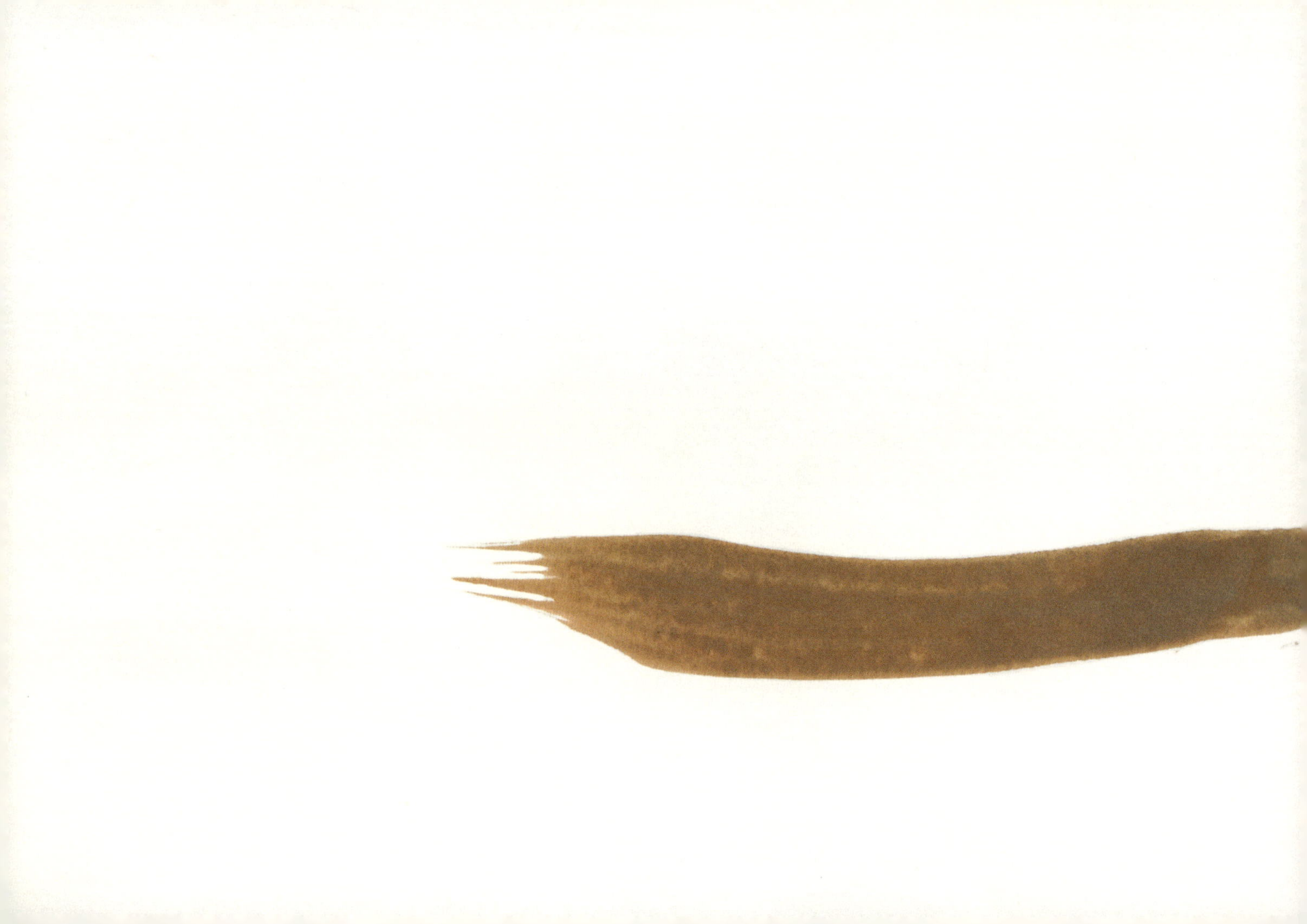

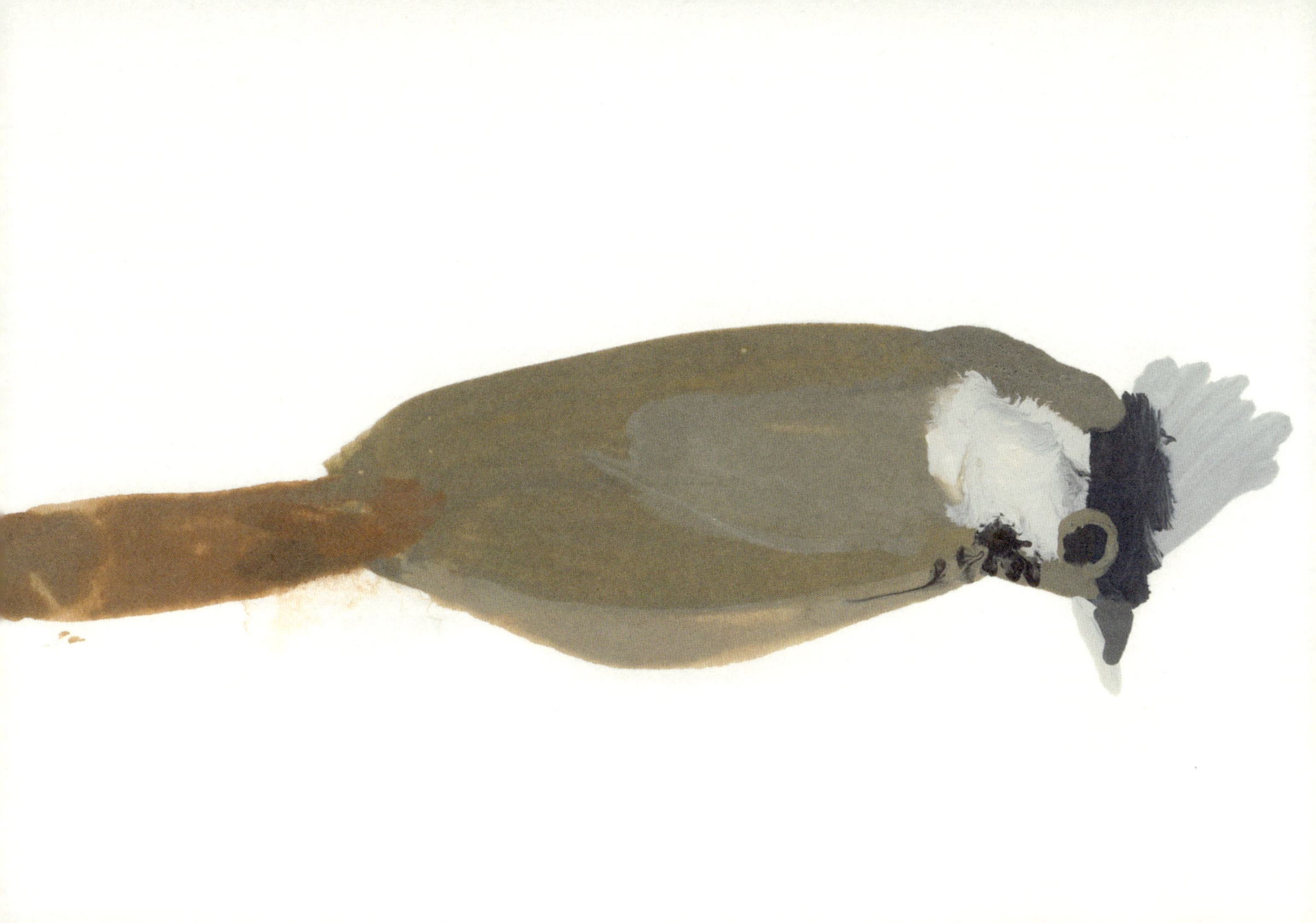

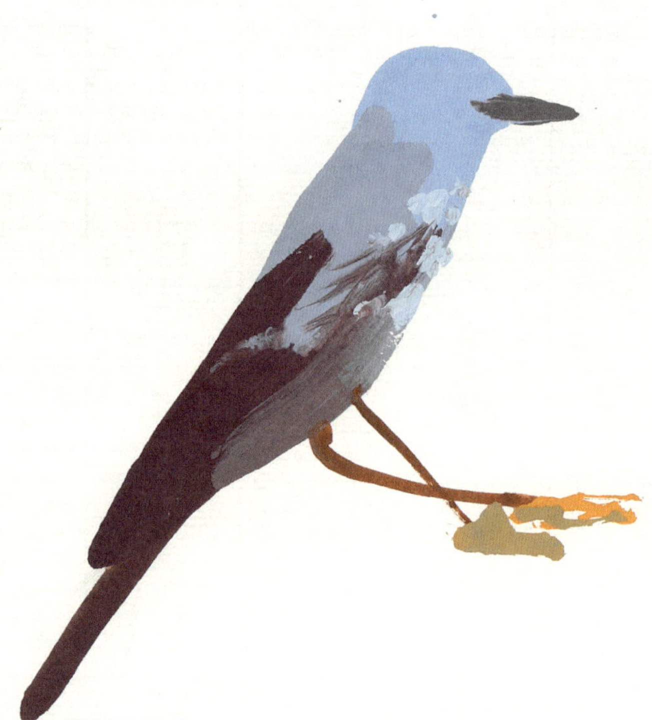

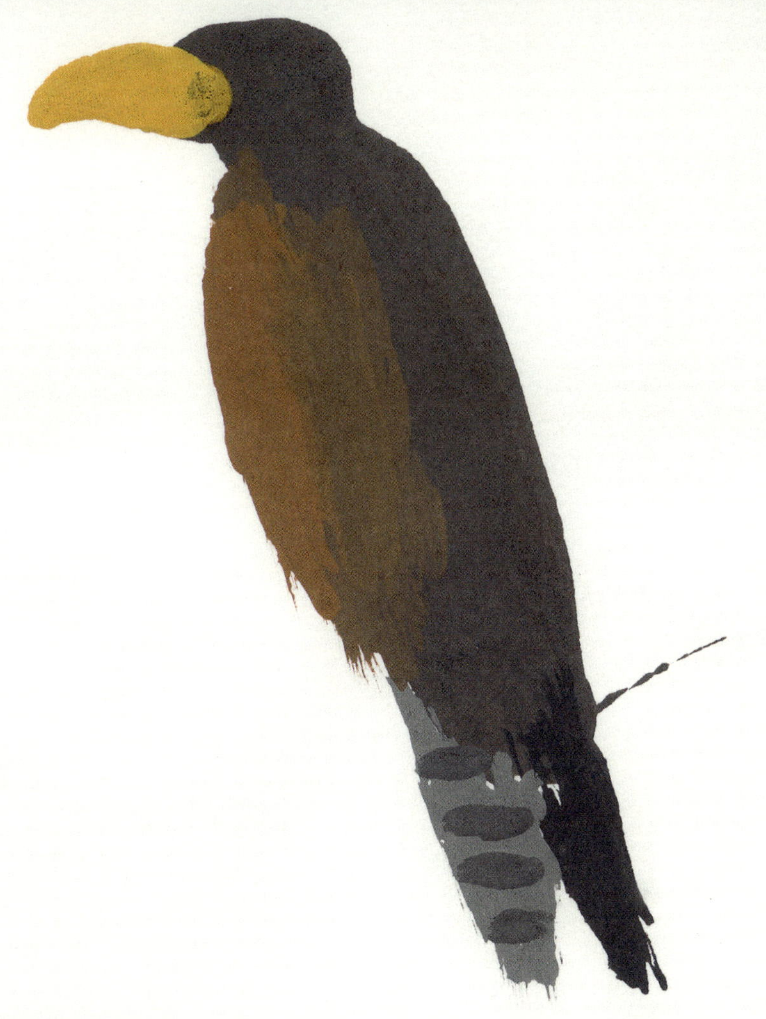

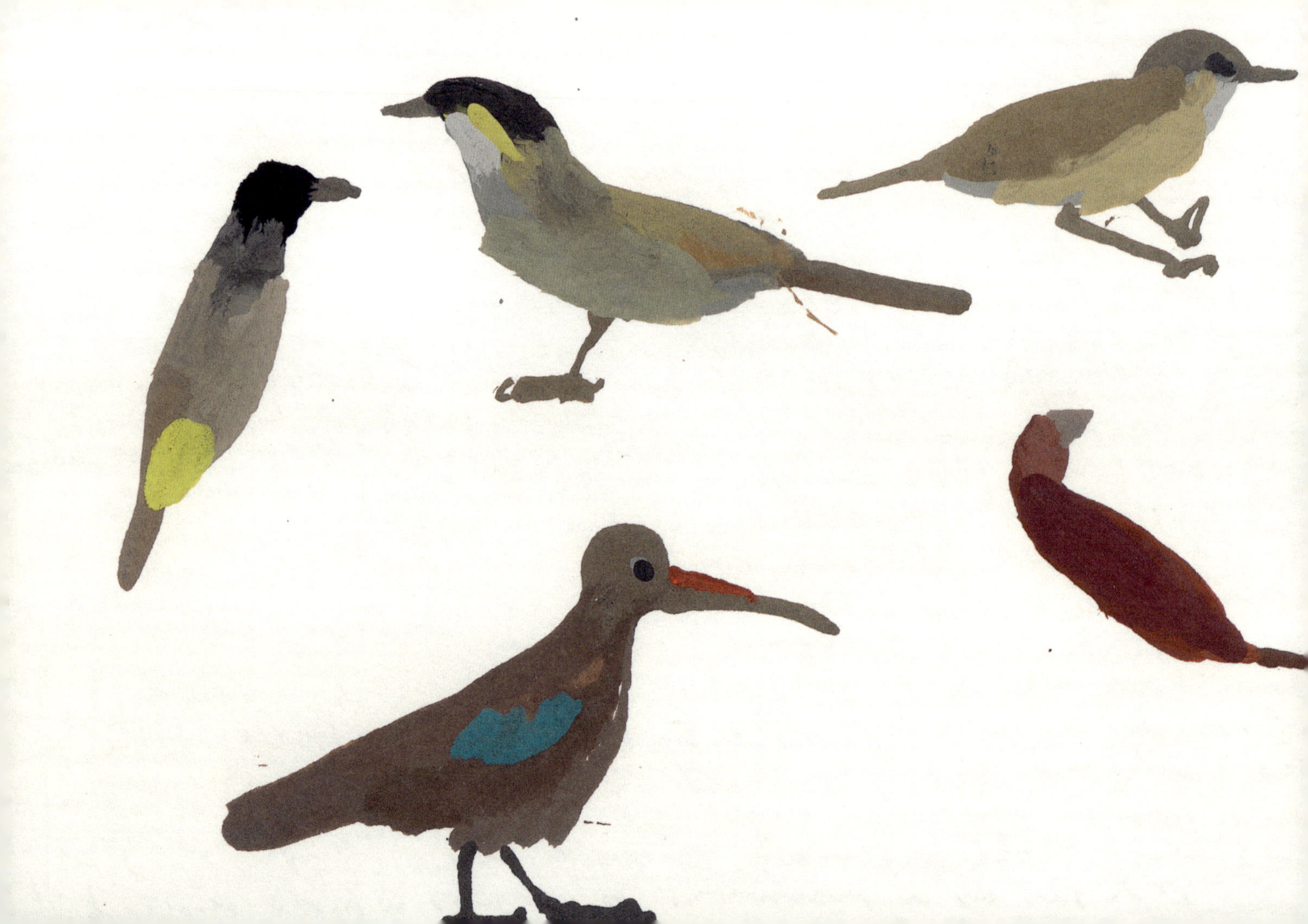

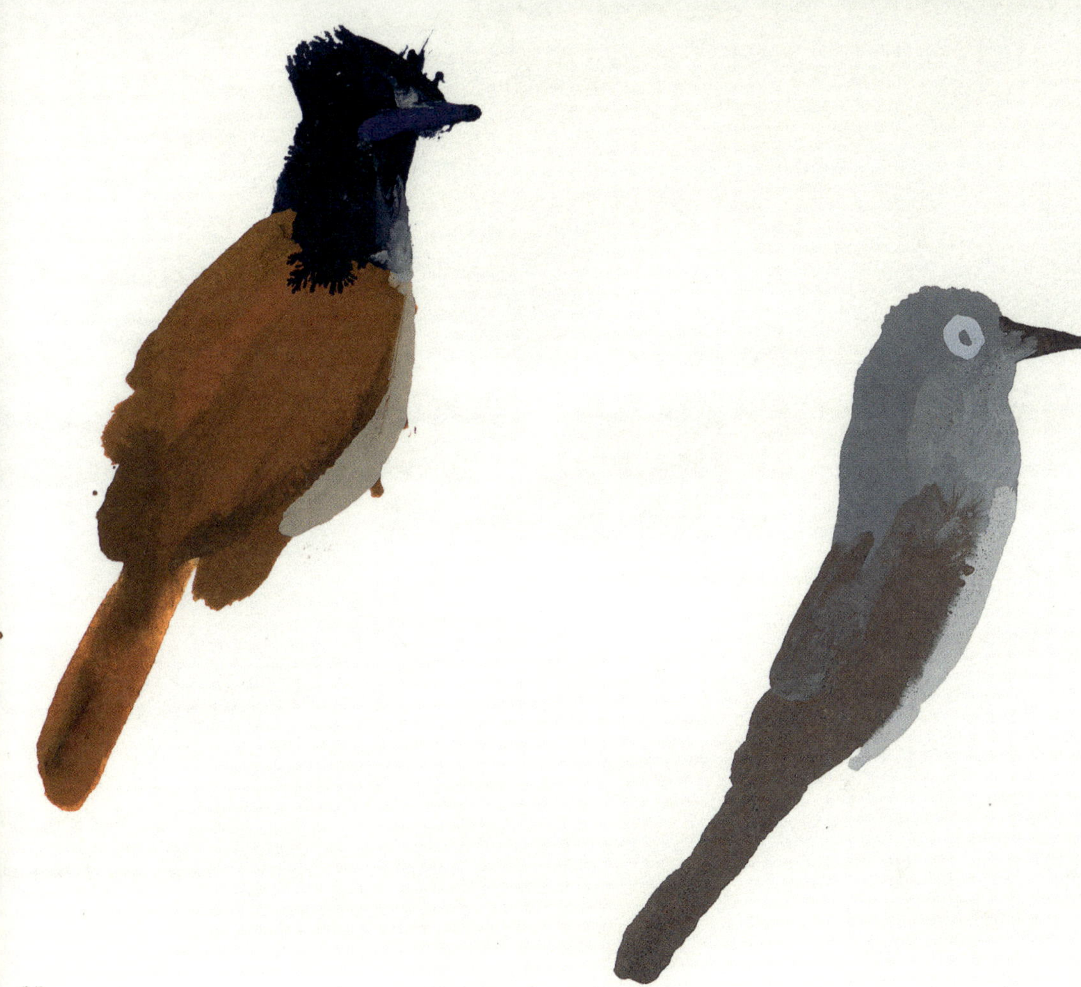

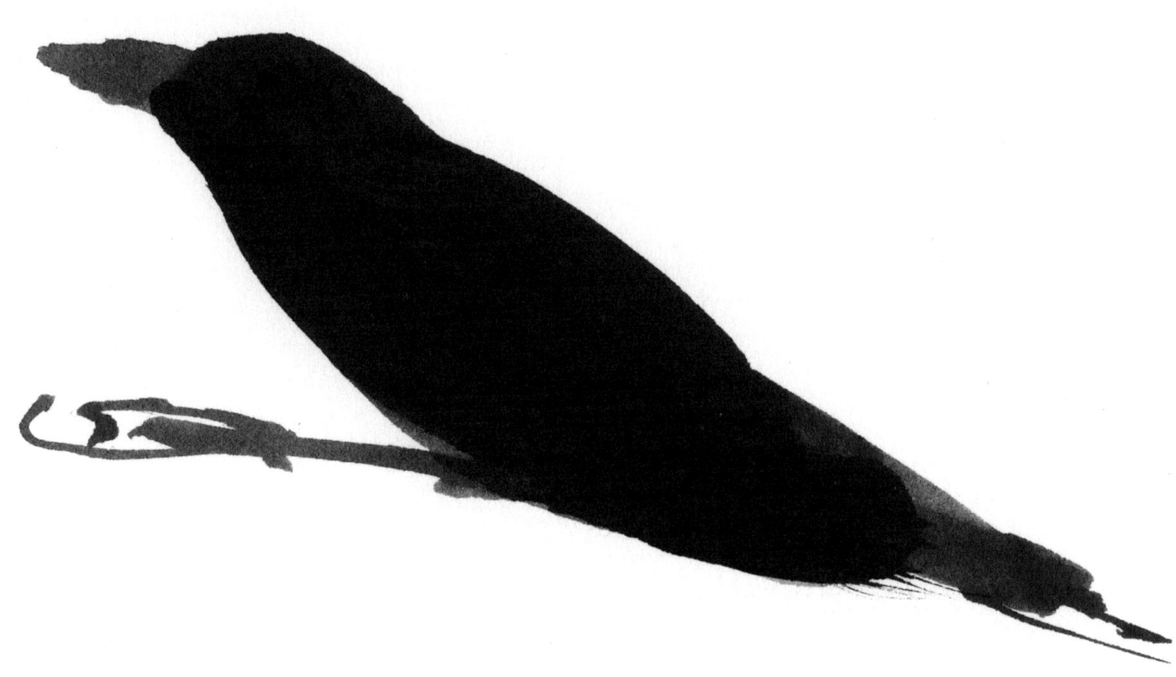

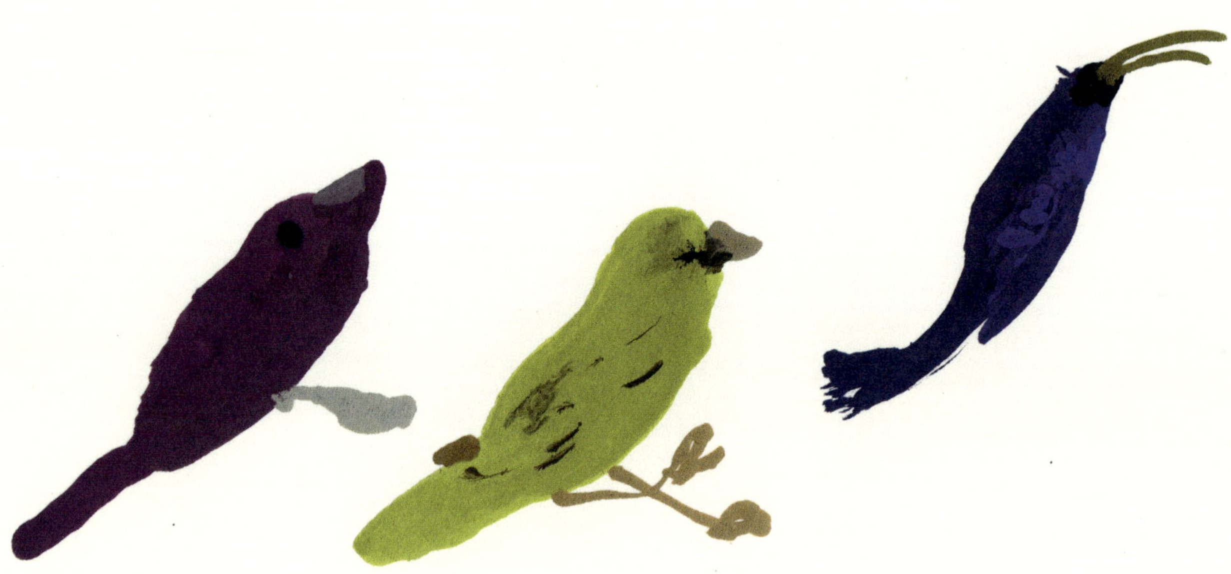

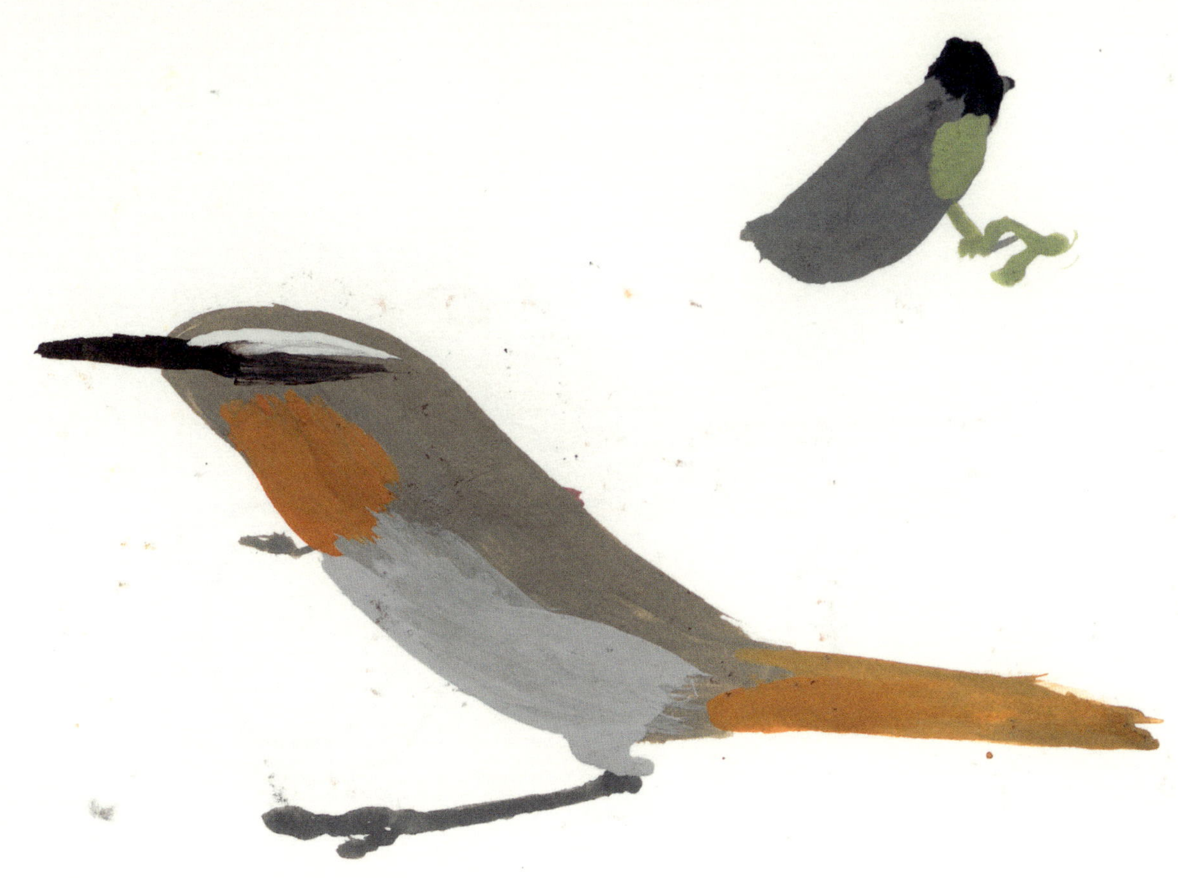

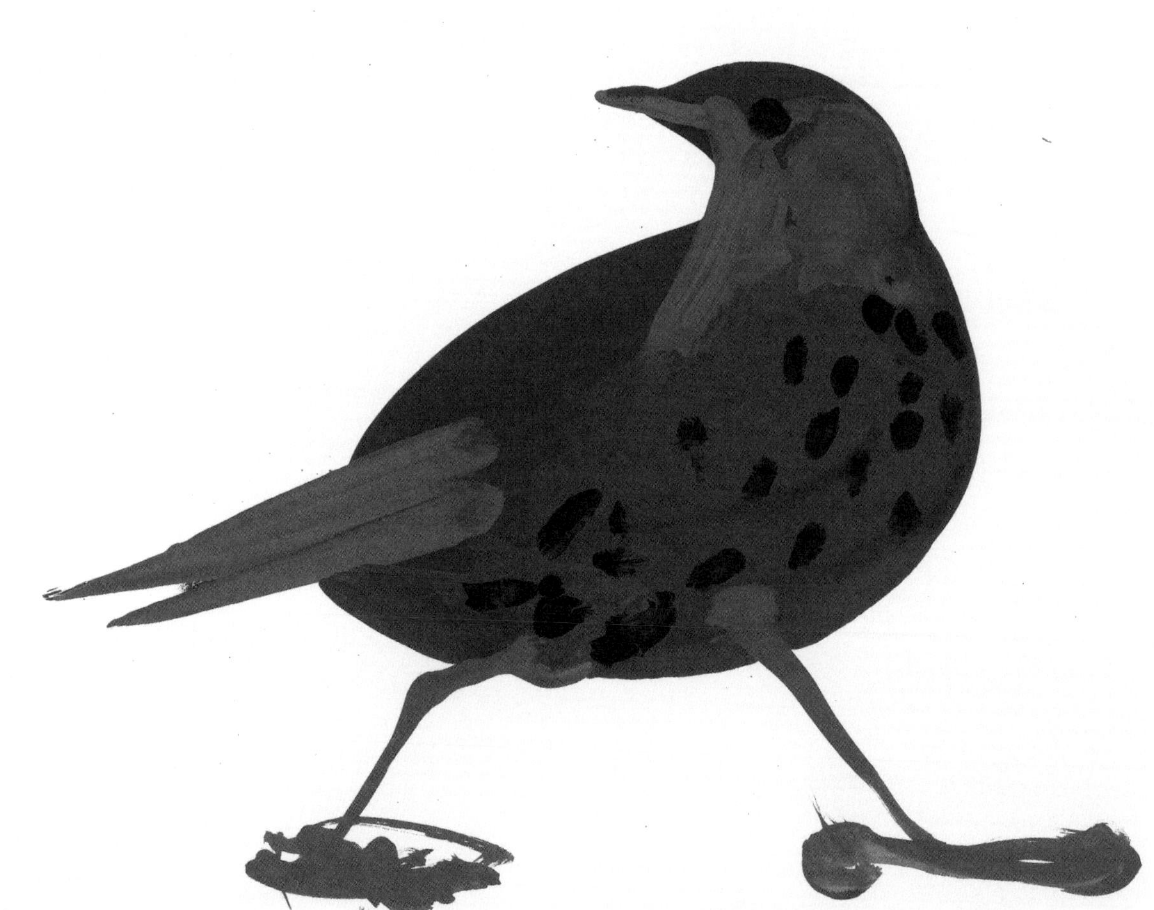

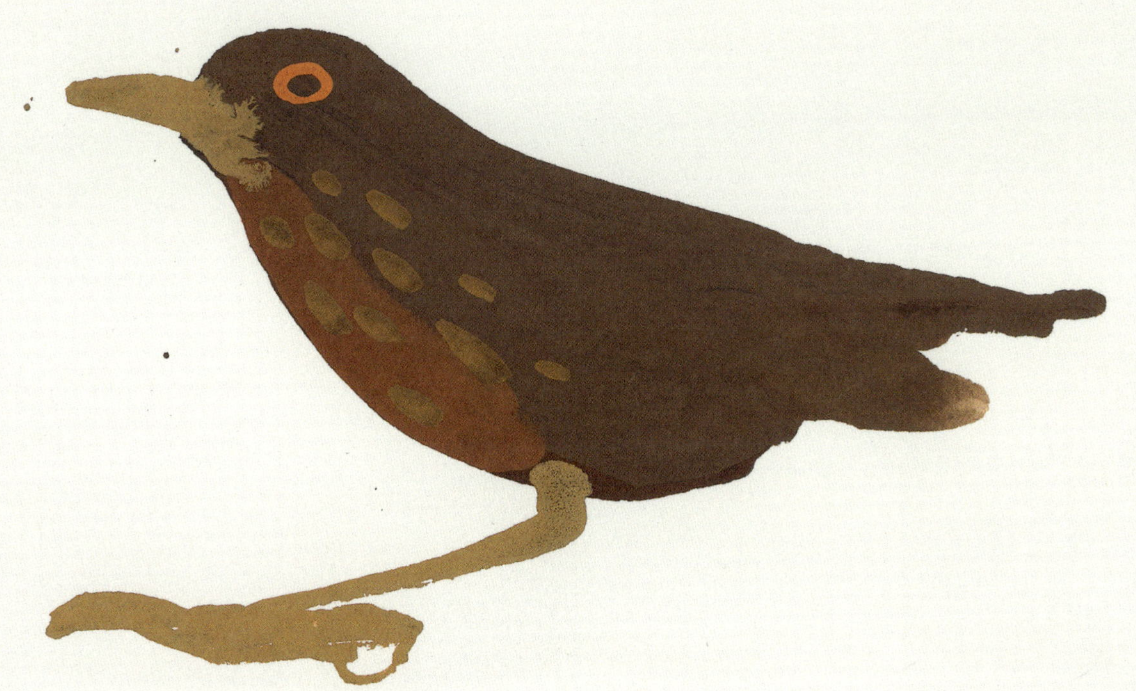

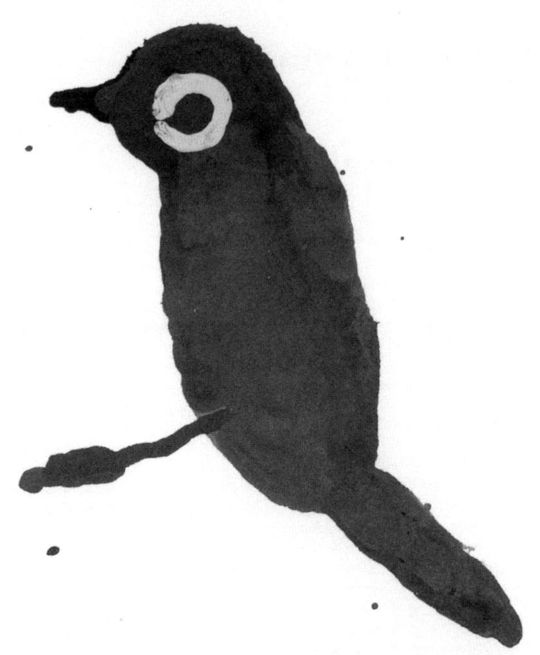

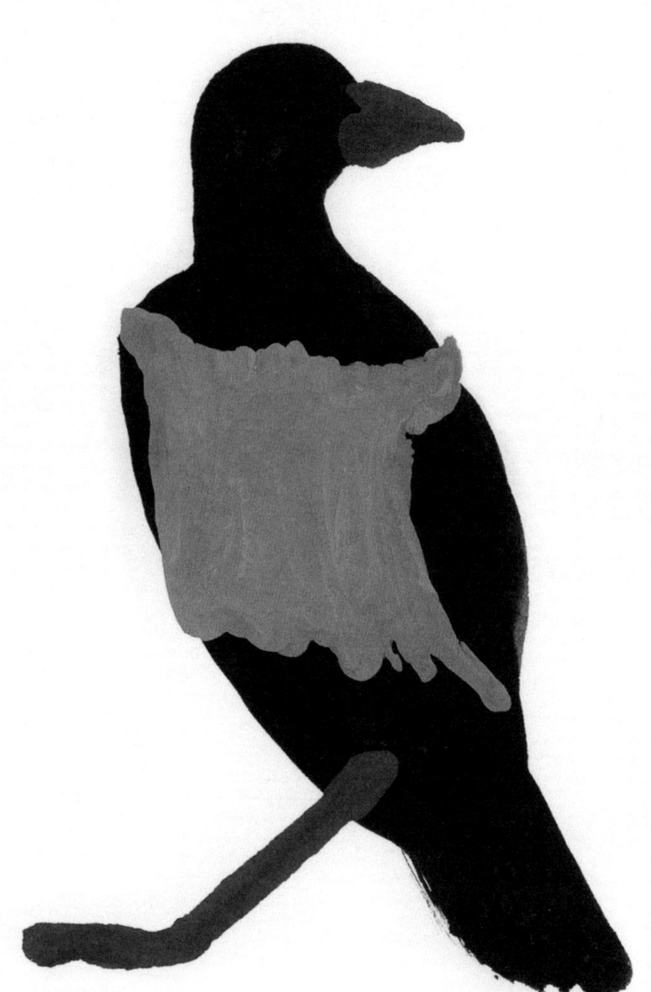

because cows milk too fatty and their digestion is not very good. It took Daphne several years to get mixture right 'trial and error' as keeper said - during which time they lost a lot of baby elephants. Off in the distance was (? Rift Valley) national park and through binocs saw zebra, impala (anyway something deer-like w blackish heads, quite big) and one buffalo. On the walk back to the main road three young warthogs crossed our path. A bit nearer gate we saw more, one was kneeling on its front knees, snuffling. As the rest came and joined him, one was swivelling in the air. They are most elegant creatures but would not win beauty competitions.

On walk home from bus stop saw sunbird, collared flycatcher and a small sparrow like bird marked like a snipe but duller. Over main gate, in acacia tree, are several sparrow-weavers nests which the weavers are building, straw by straw. They hang from dangling branches - the nests - you wonder how they get the first straws to grip.

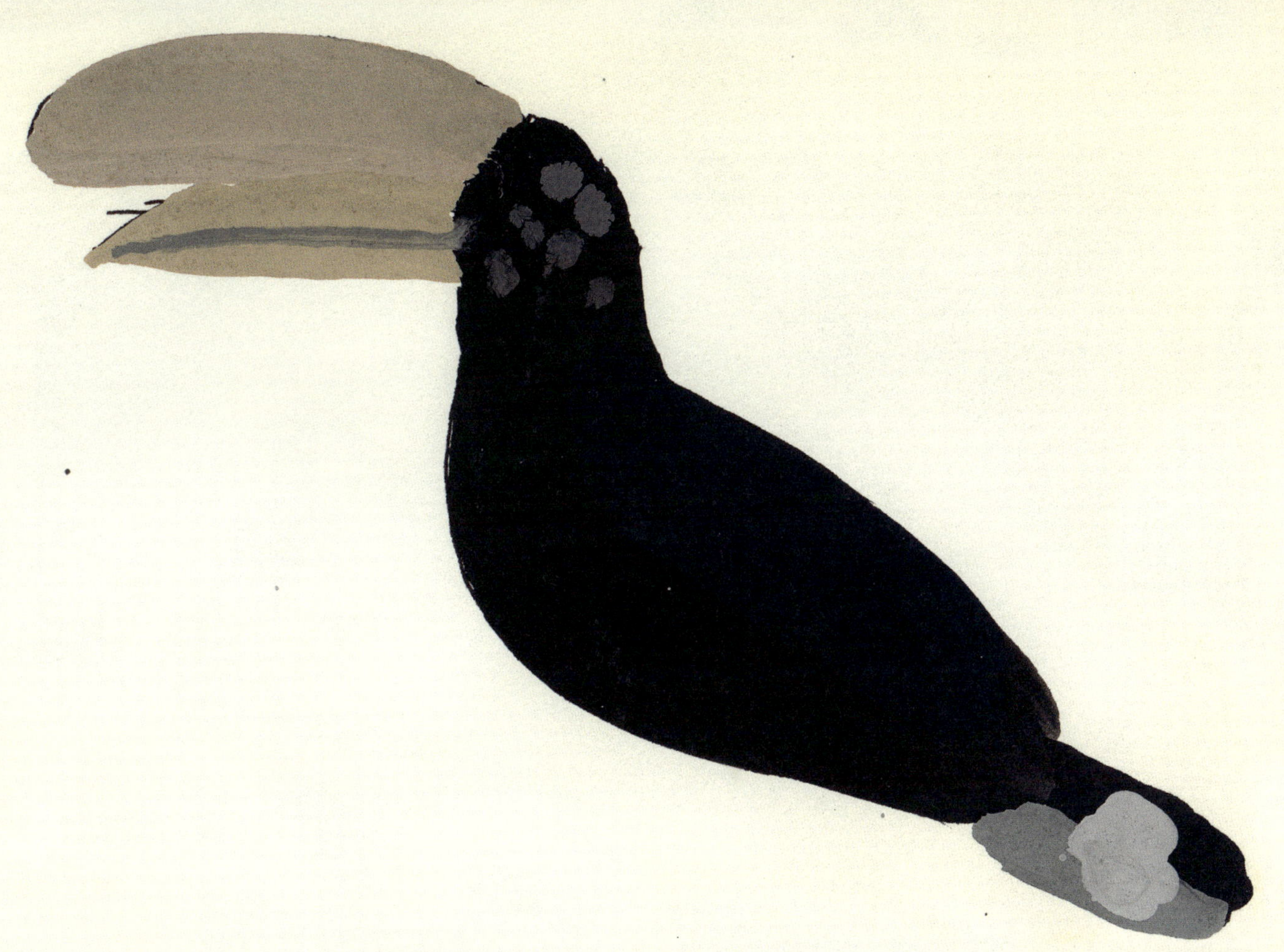

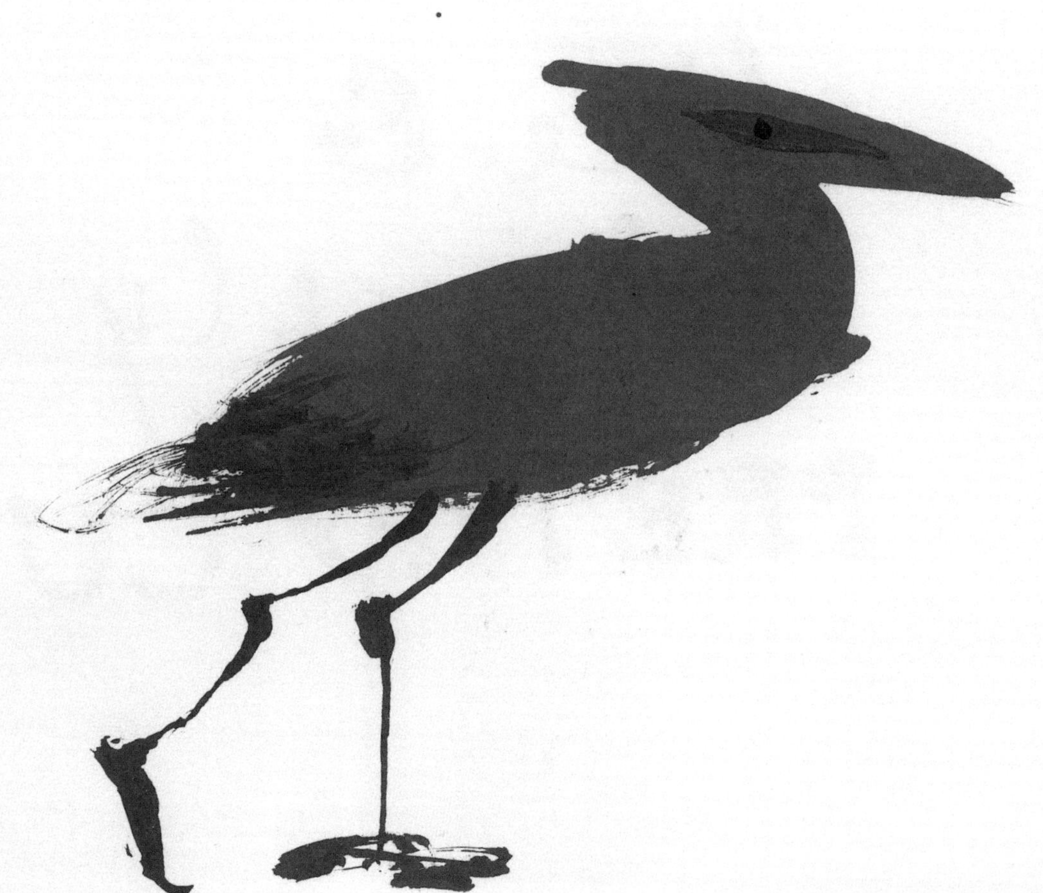

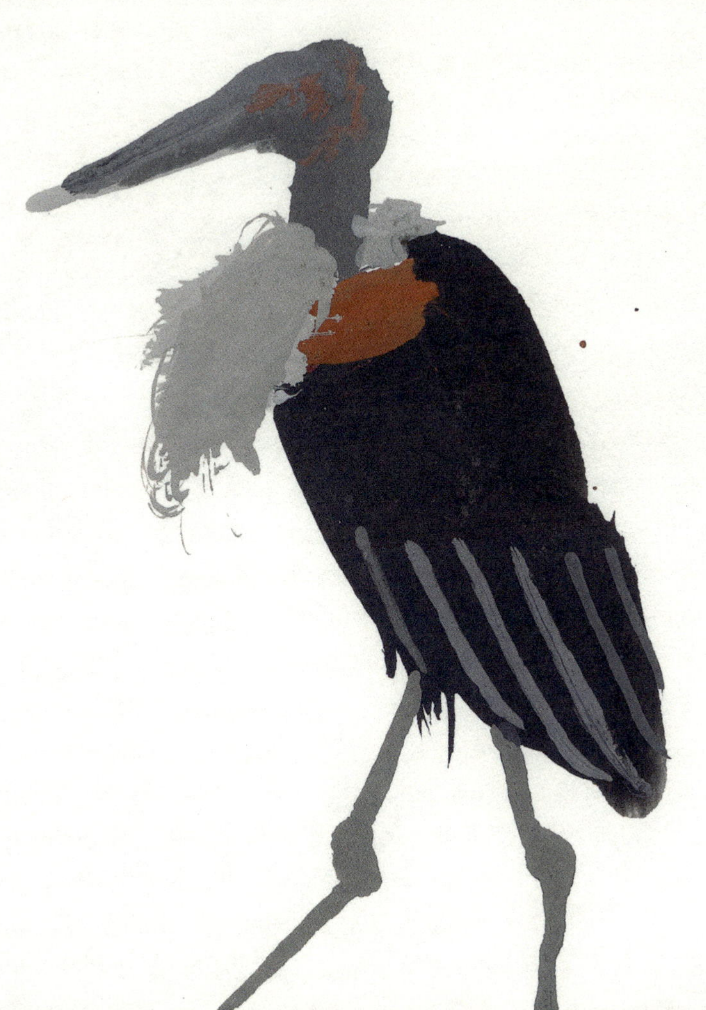

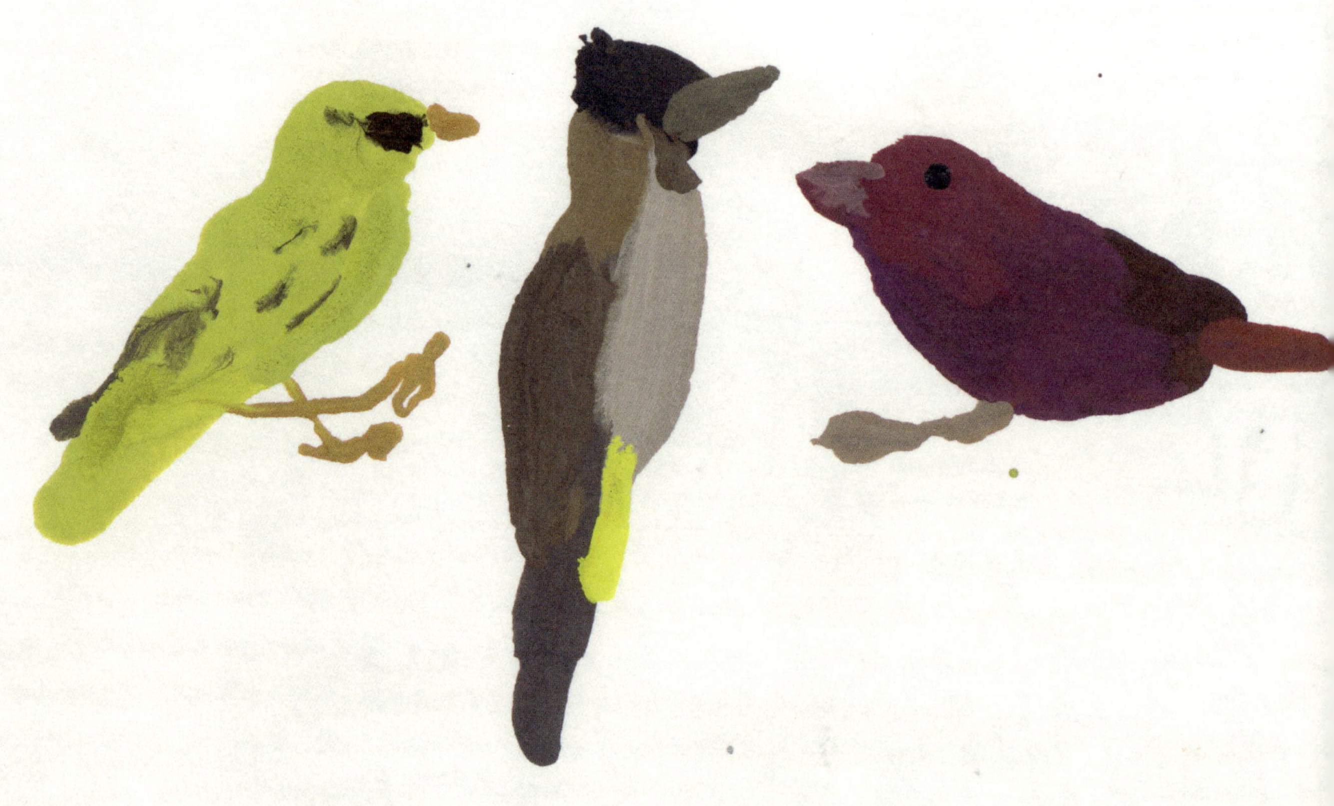

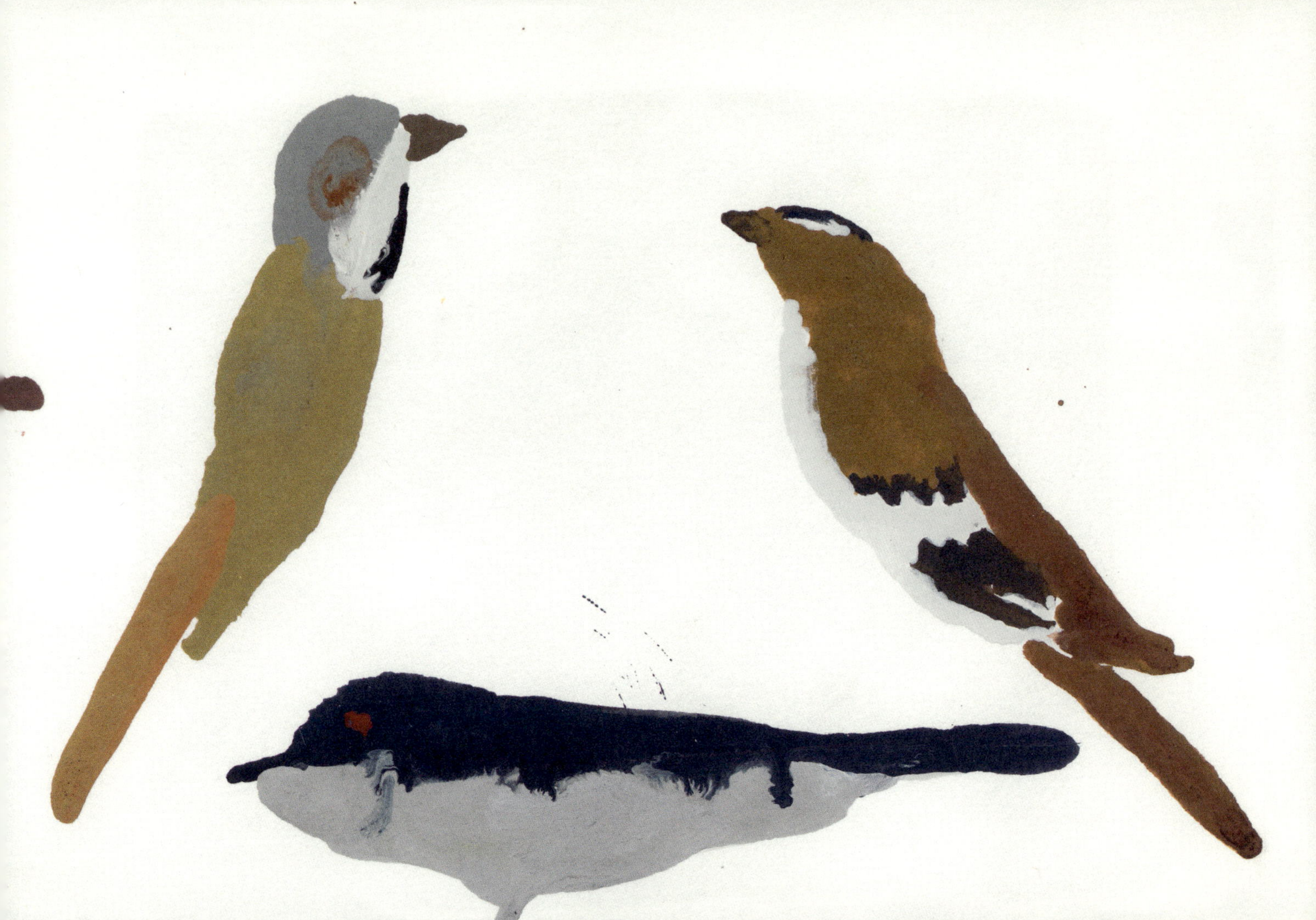

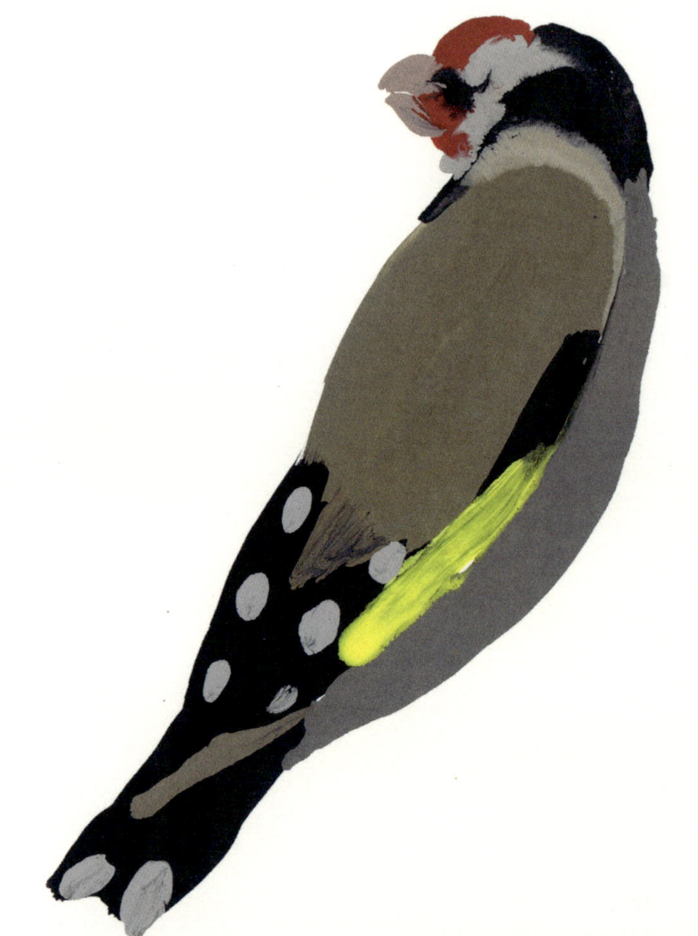

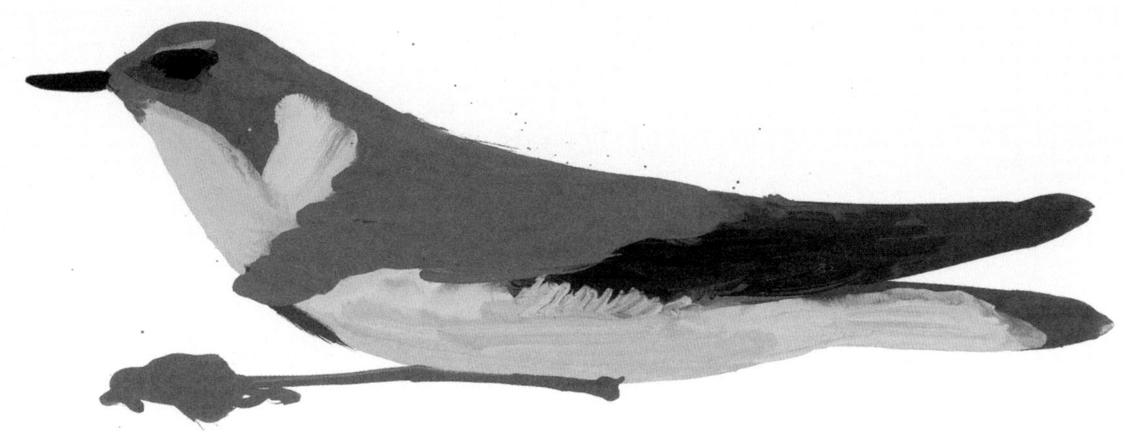

Dawson City 140804
Worlaby (Maxinecarr)
Hawkstow (where Stubbs drew Anatomy of a horse)
Barrow on Humber
Black tailed Godwit
green Sandpiper
Sand martin
Gtr black backed gull
P&O Pride of Hull
.. Pride of Bruges
Turnstone
common gull
Black headed gull
Whitethroat
Linnet

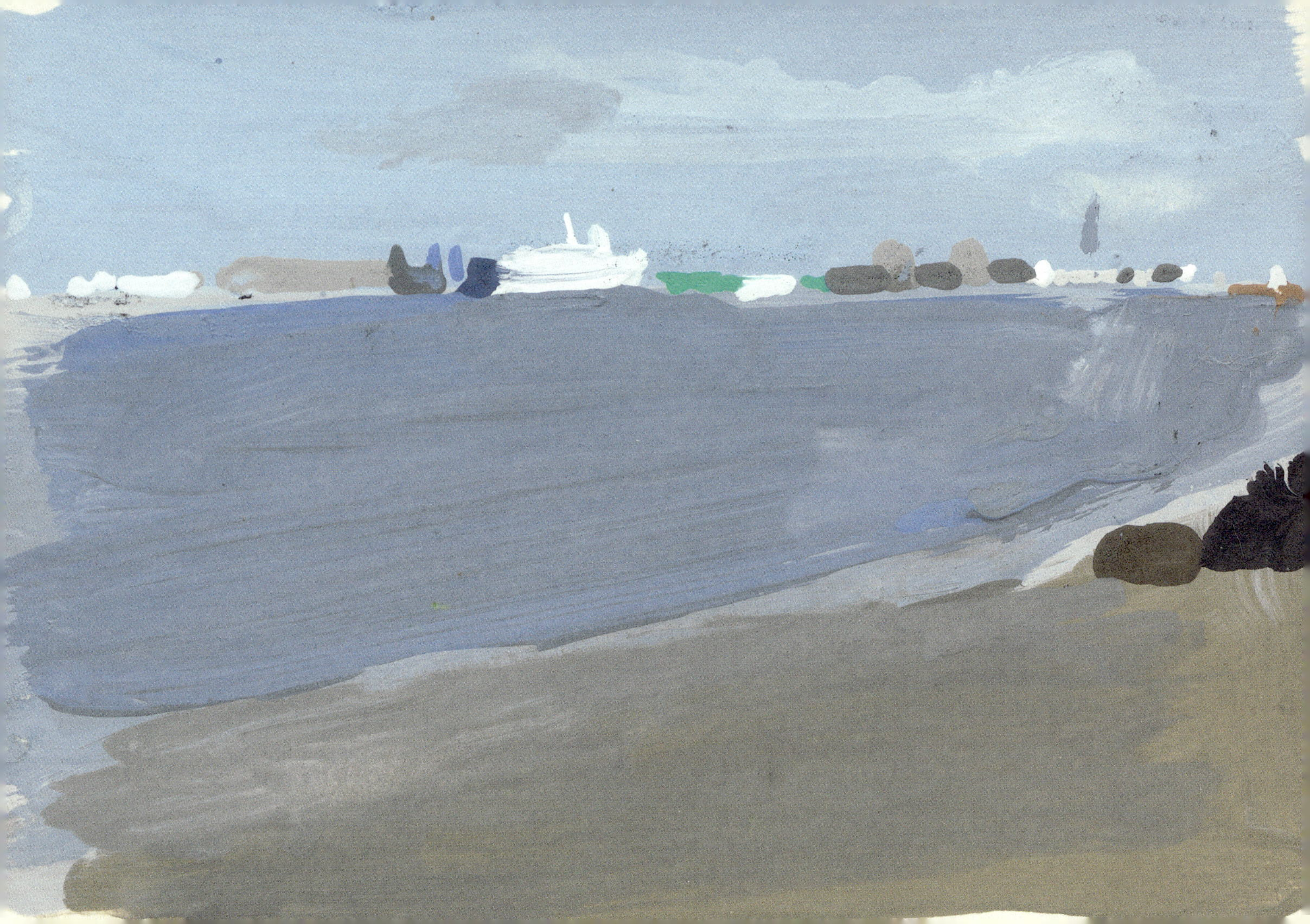

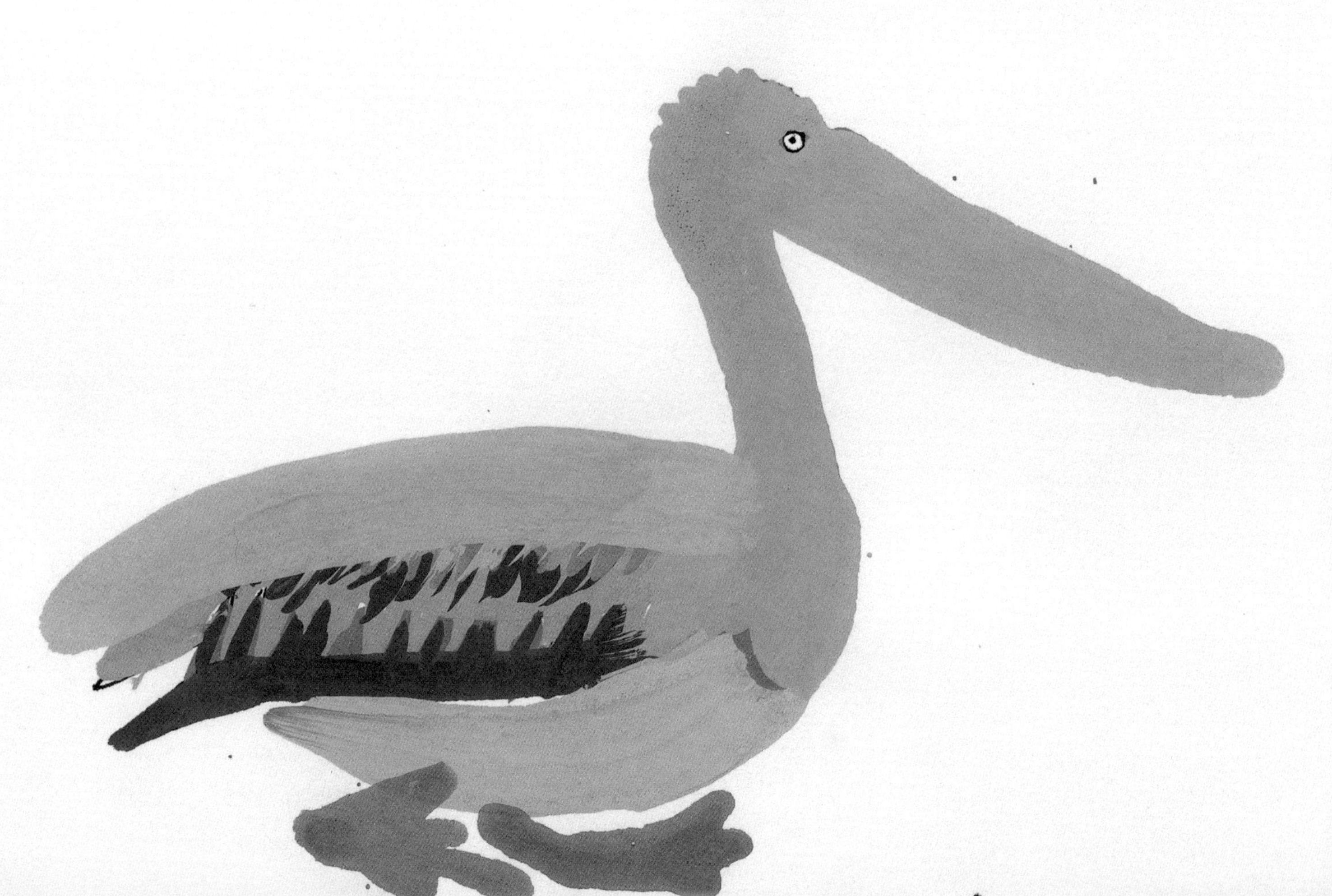

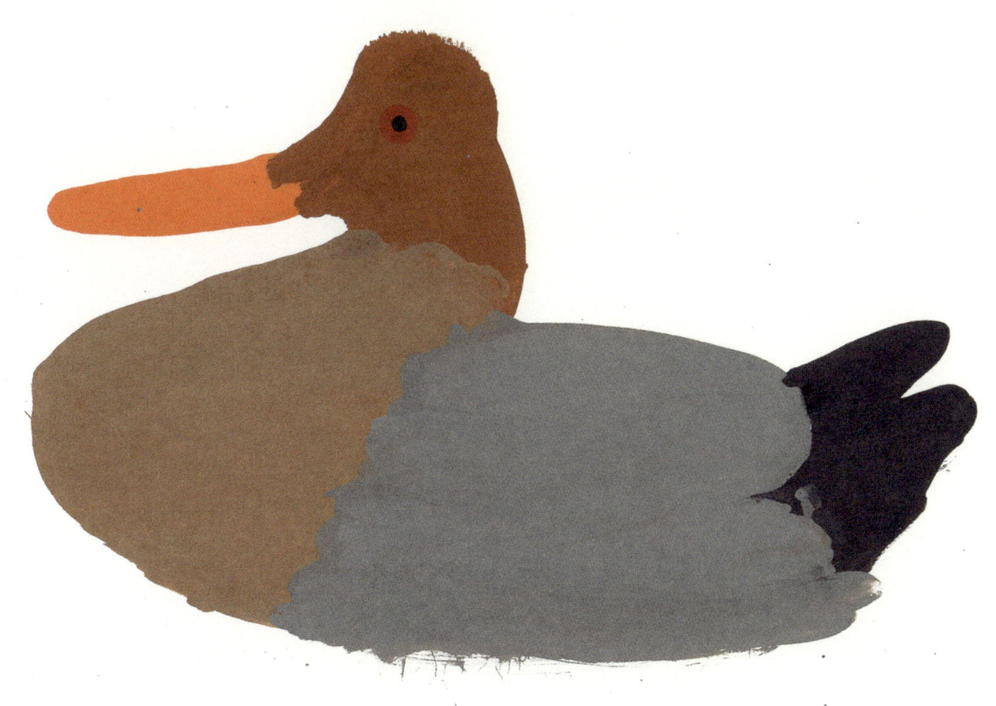

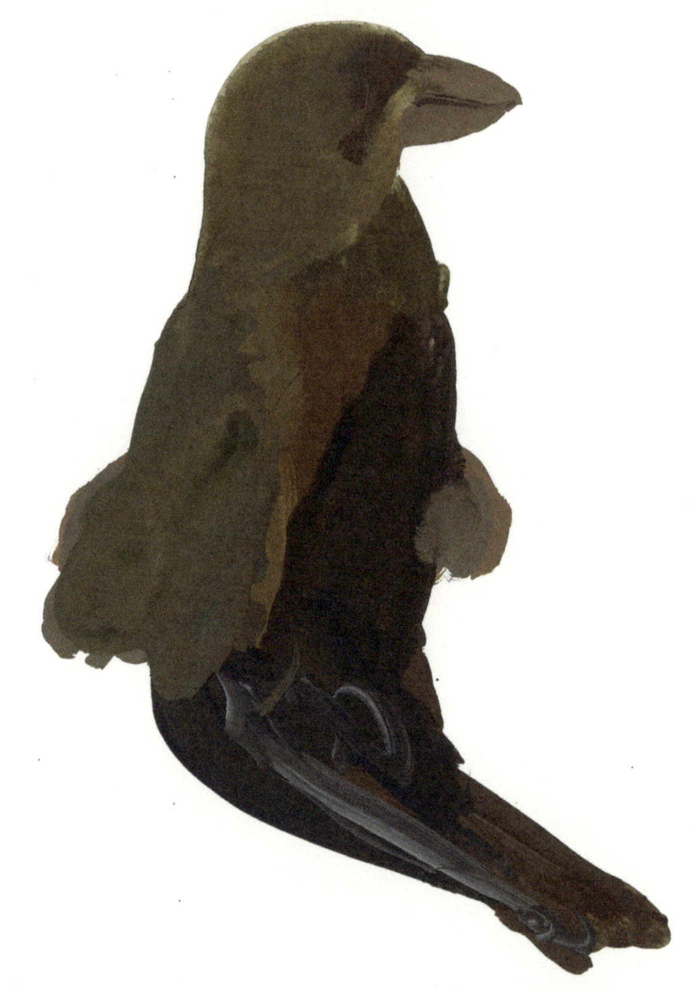

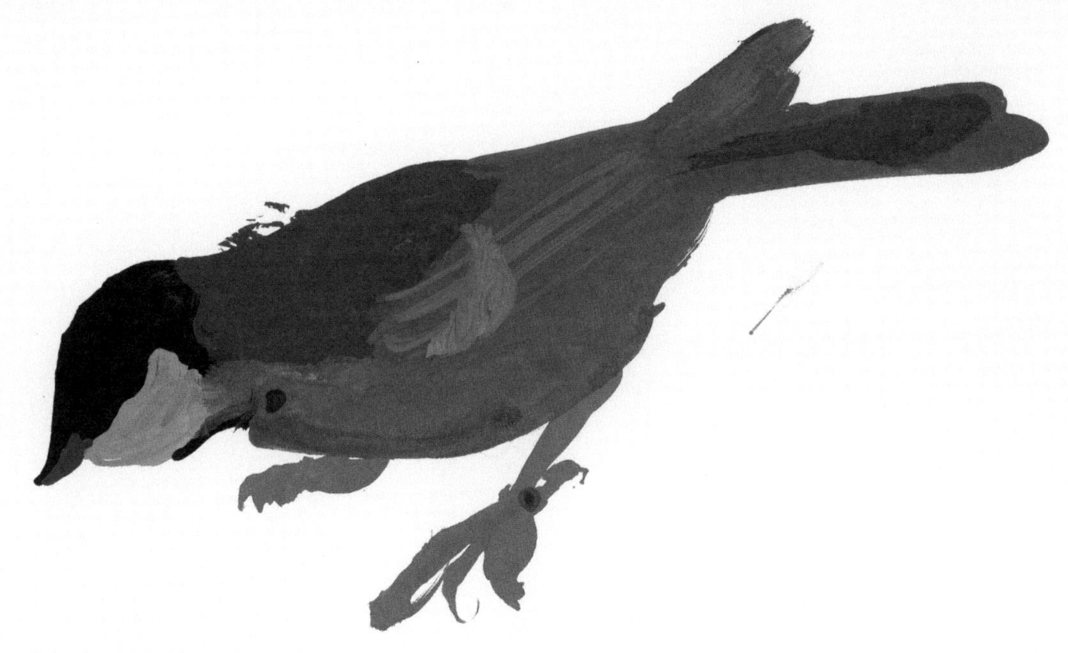

a turtle dove, also for a short time on the telegraph pole a goshawk.

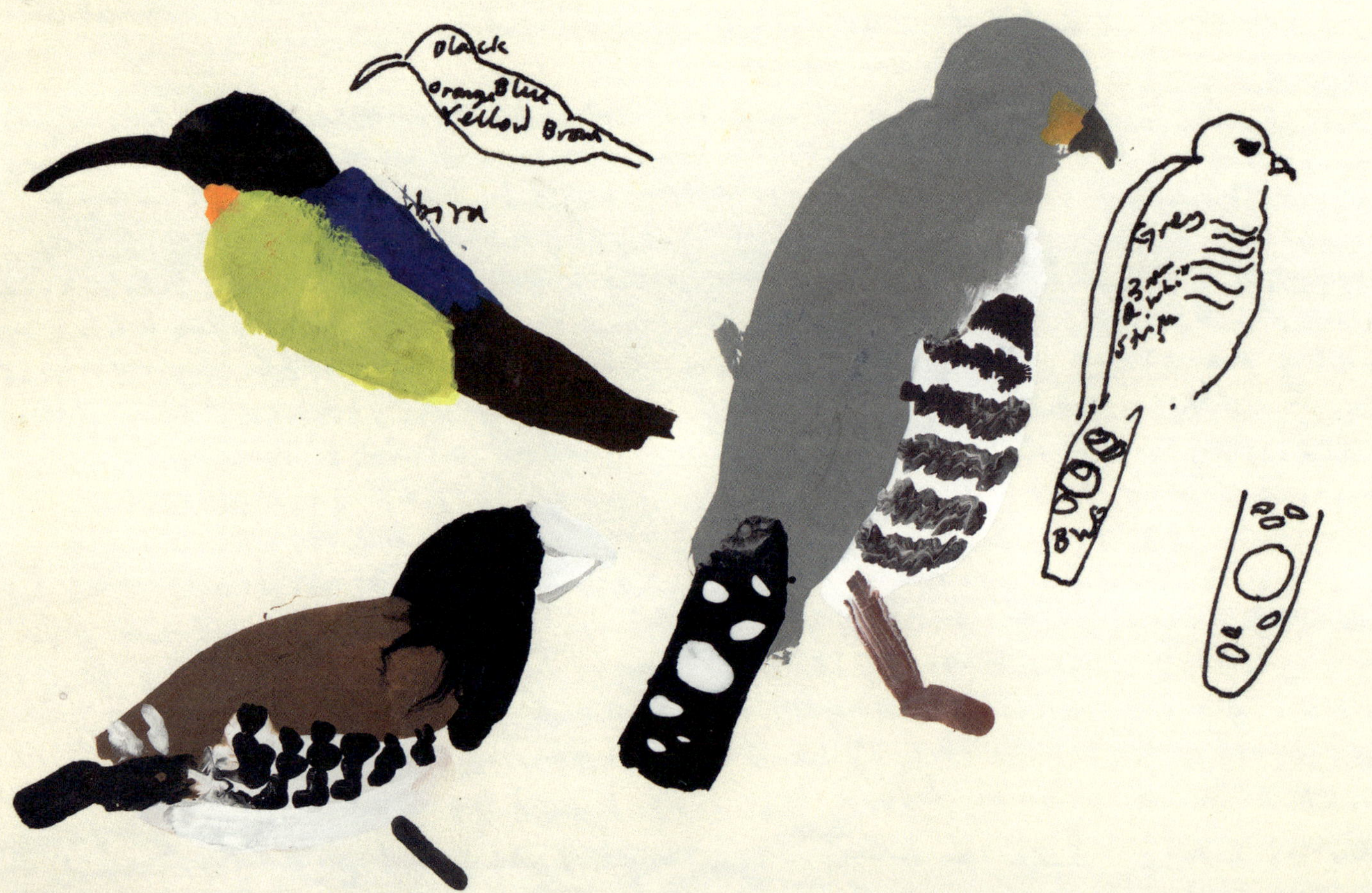

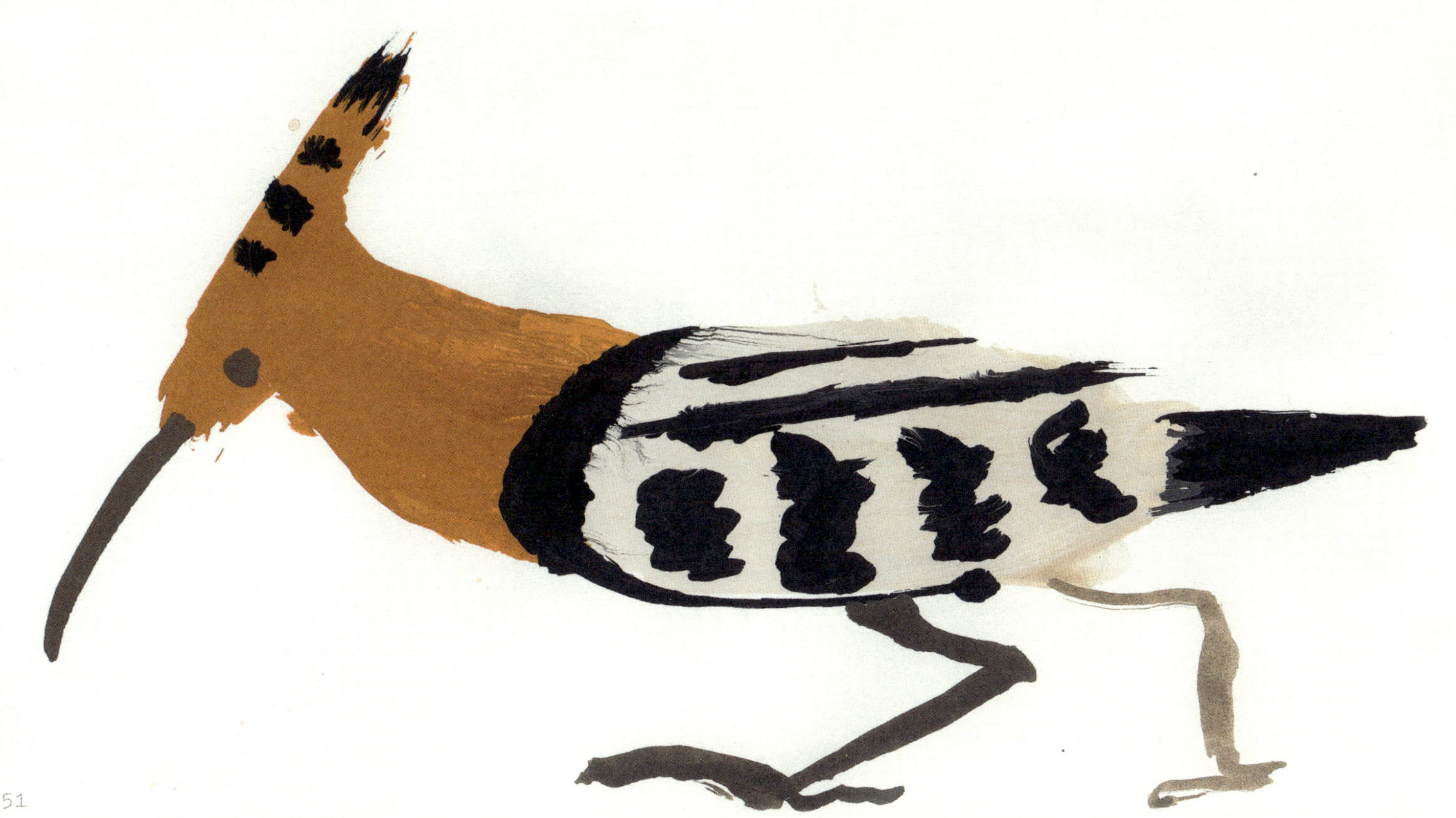

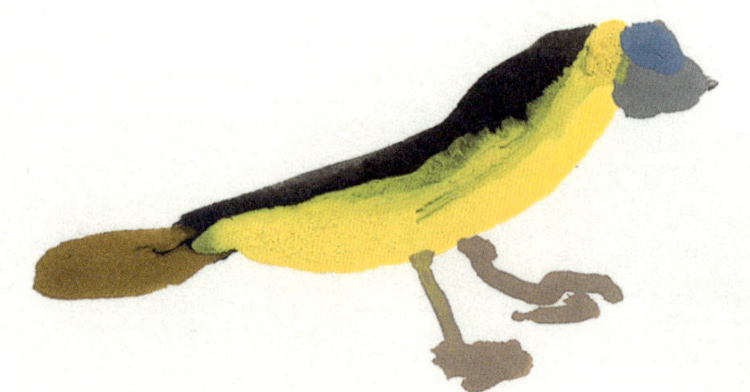

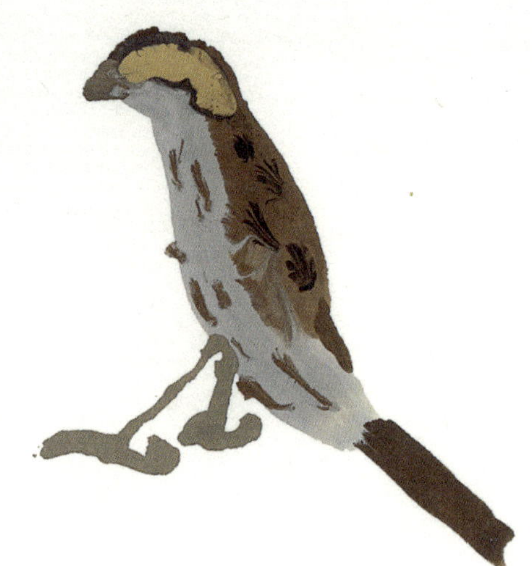

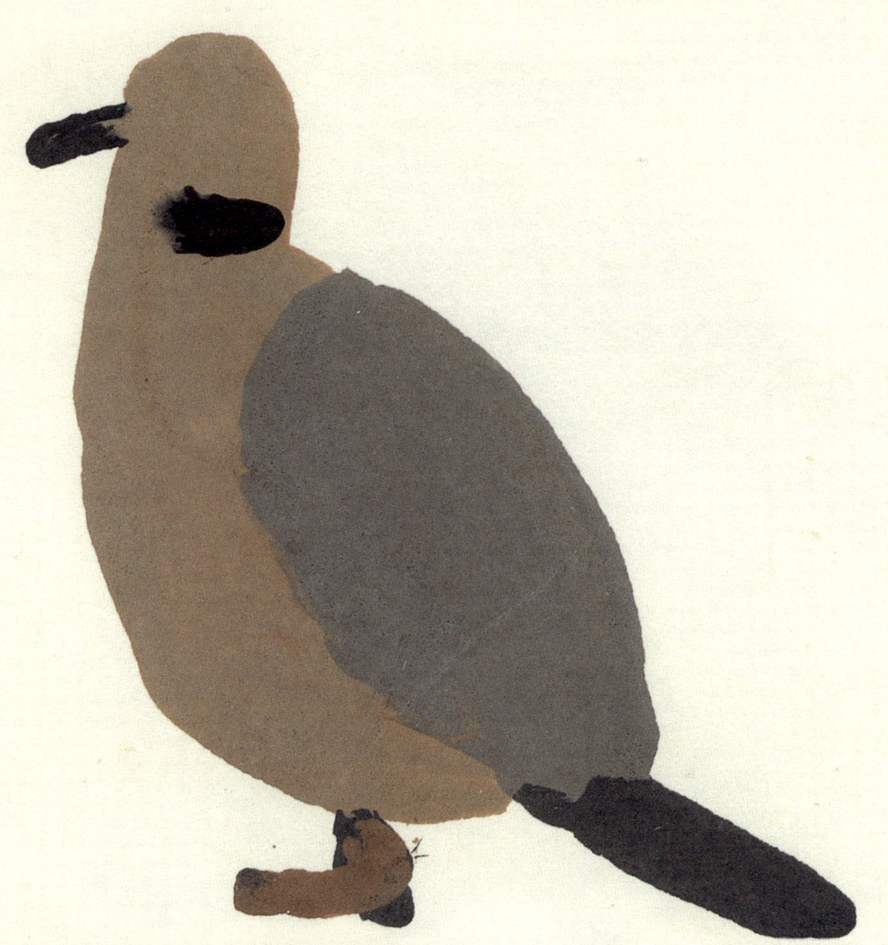

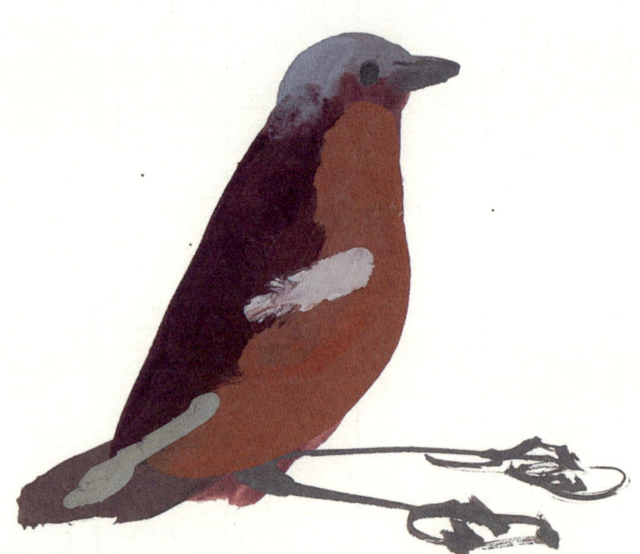

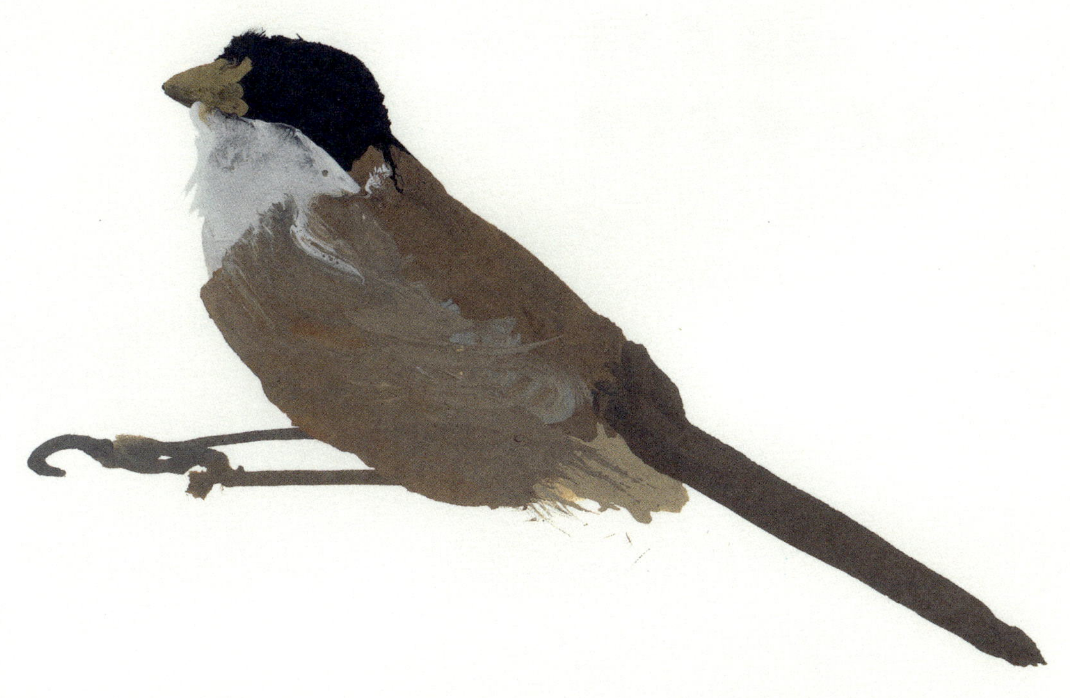

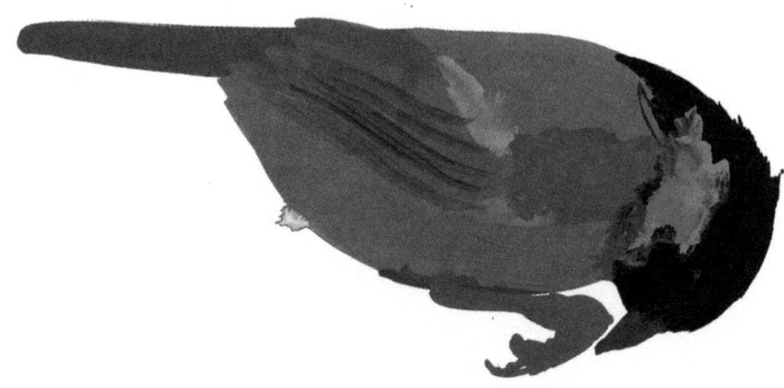

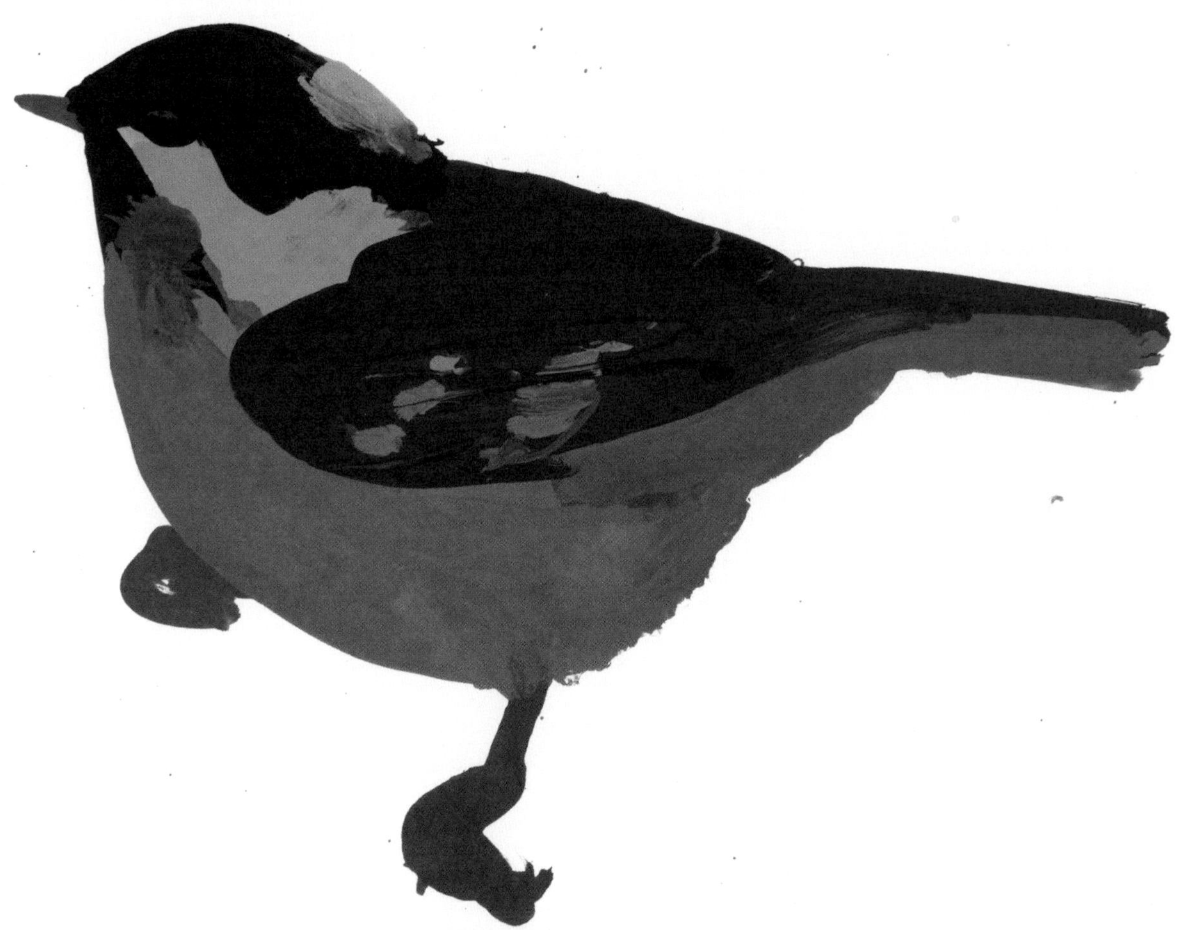

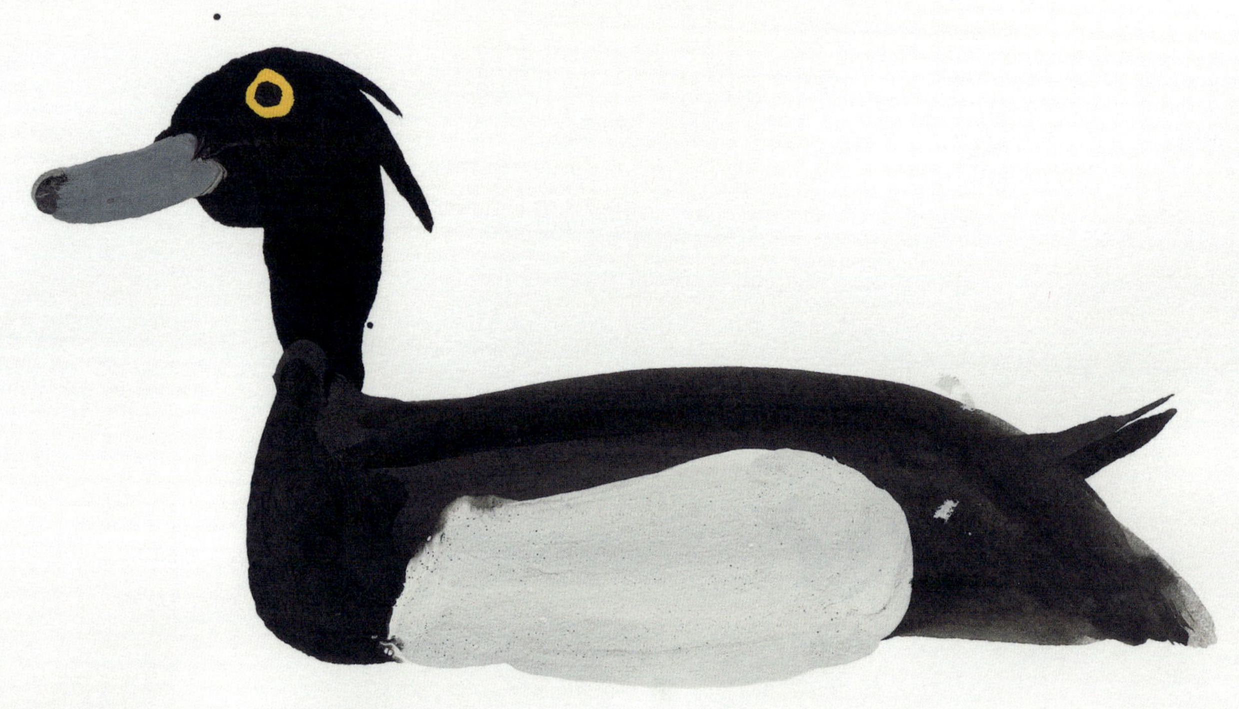

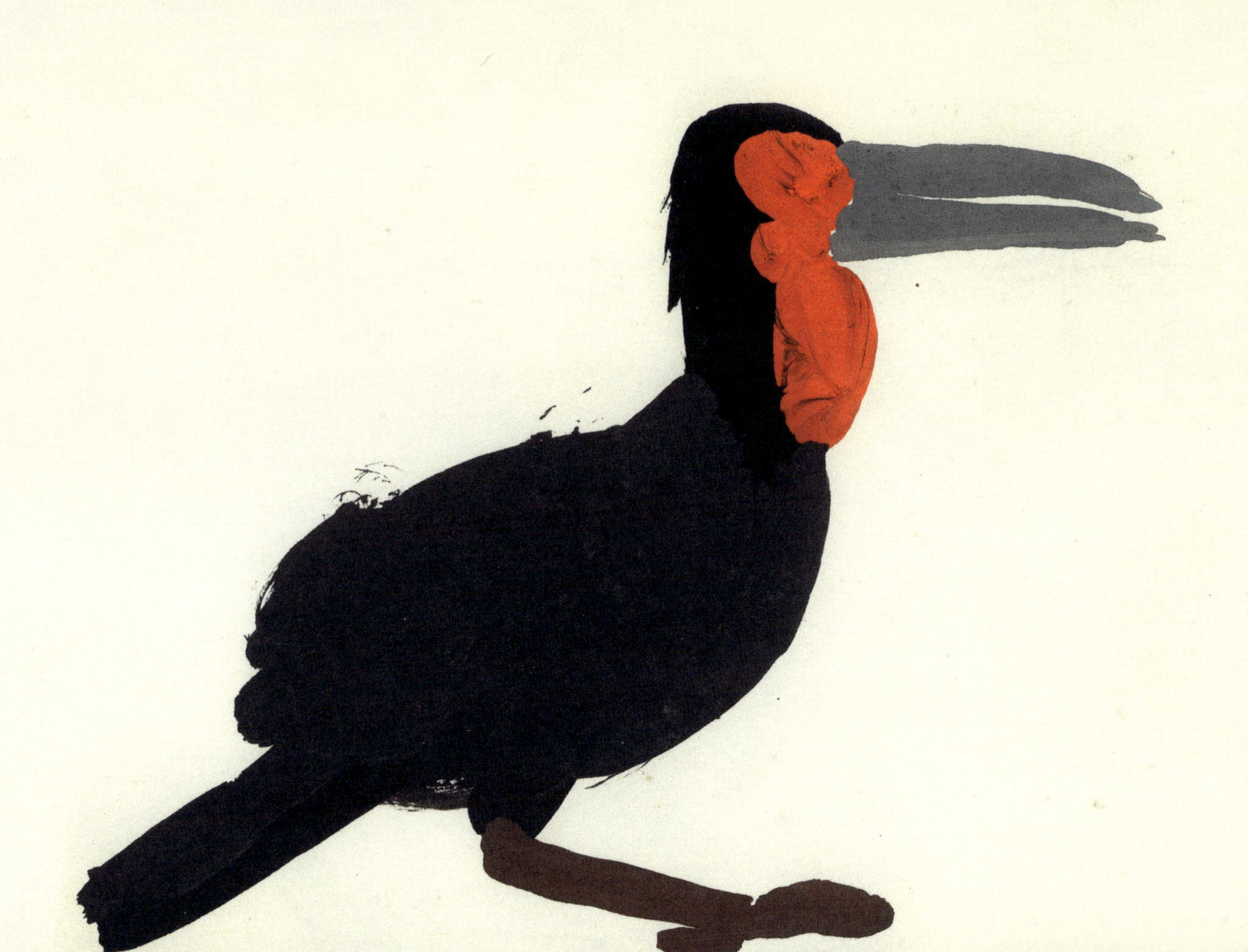

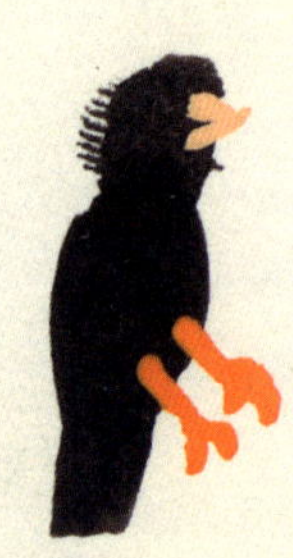

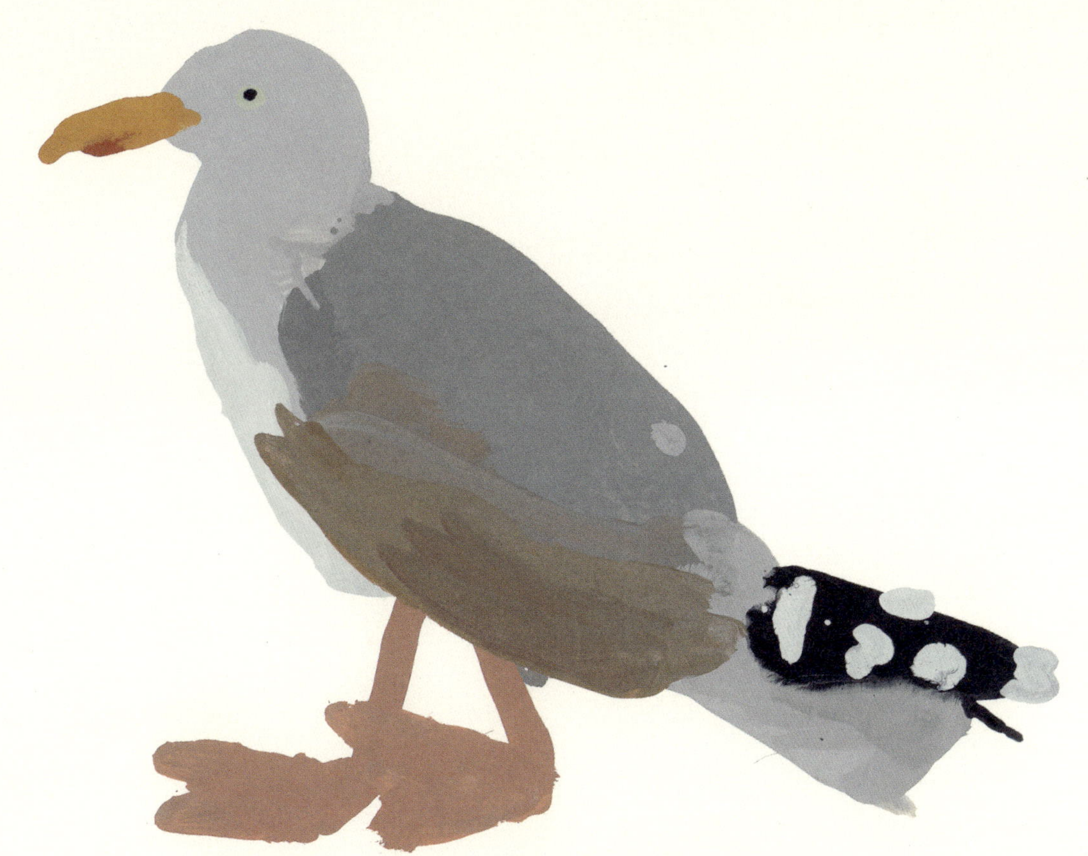

Index of bird species

41 House sparrow, Black-throated wattle-eye, White-browed sparrow-weaver

42 Goldfinch

43 Sand martin

44 Moorhen

45 The Humber at Hull

46 Pink-backed pelican

47 Pochard

48 Greenfinch

49 Great tit

50 Collared sunbird, African goshawks

51 Hoopoe

52 Yellow-rumped tinkerbird, Streaky seedeater

53 Ring-necked dove

54 Chaffinch

55 Blackcap

56 Great tit

57 Coal tit

58 Tufted duck

59 Southern ground hornbill

60 Village indigo bird

61 Herring gull

Royal Academy Publications
Florence Dassonville, Production Co-ordinator
Alison Hissey, Project Editor
Carola Krueger, Production Manager
Peter Sawbridge, Editorial Director
Nick Tite, Publisher

Design: Rebecca Penmore
Typeset in: Pitch
Colour origination: DawkinsColour Ltd

Printed in Wales by Gomer Press

Photography by Mike Bruce

British Library Cataloguing-in-Publication Data
A catalogue record for this book is available from the British Library

ISBN 978-1-912520-37-4
ISBN 978-1-912520-54-1 (special edition)

Distributed outside the United States and Canada by ACC Art Books Ltd, Sandy Lane, Old Martlesham, Woodbridge, Suffolk IP12 4SD

Distributed in the United States and Canada by ARTBOOK | D.A.P., 75 Broad Street, Suite 630, New York, NY 10004